Gay, Lesbian, Bisexual, & Transgender Myths

from the Arapaho to the Zuñi

American Indian Studies

Vol. 13

PETER LANG
New York • Washington, D.C./Baltimore • Bern
Frankfurt am Main • Berlin • Brussels • Vienna • Oxford

Gay, Lesbian, Bisexual, & Transgender Myths from the Arapaho to the Zuñi

AN ANTHOLOGY

EDITED BY

Jim Elledge

PETER LANG
New York • Washington, D.C./Baltimore • Bern
Frankfurt am Main • Berlin • Brussels • Vienna • Oxford

Library of Congress Cataloging-in-Publication Data

Names: Elledge, Jim, editor.
Title: Gay, lesbian, bisexual, and transgender myths from the Arapaho to the Zuñi: an anthology / edited by Jim Elledge.
Description: New York: Peter Lang, 2002.
Series: American Indian studies; v. 13 | 1058-563X
Includes bibliographical references.
Identifiers: LCCN 2001029725 | ISBN 978-0-8204-5286-9 (paperback: alk. paper)
Subjects: LCSH: Indian mythology—North America. Homosexuality—Mythology. Creation—Mythology. Two-spirit people—Folklore. Gay men—Folklore. Lesbians—Folklore. Legends—North America.
Classification: LCC E98.R3 G38 2002 | DDC 398.2/089/97
LC record available at https://lccn.loc.gov/2001029725

Bibliographic information published by **Die Deutsche Nationalbibliothek**. **Die Deutsche Nationalbibliothek** lists this publication in the "Deutsche Nationalbibliografie"; detailed bibliographic data are available on the Internet at http://dnb.d-nb.de/.

Cover design by Lisa Dillon

Cover photograph by John H. Fouch, 1877, courtesy of Dr. James S. Brust. The individual on the left is the Crow *boté,* or male two-spirit, Osh-Tish ("Finds Them and Kills Them"), also called "Squaw Jim." The individual on the right may be, according to some scholars, the female two-spirit The Other Magpie, who was Osh-Tish's companion in the Battle of Rosebud.

The paper in this book meets the guidelines for permanence and durability of the Committee on Production Guidelines for Book Longevity of the Council of Library Resources.

29 Broadway, 18th floor, New York, NY 10006
www.peterlang.com

Printed in the United States of America

For David

I, I am happy, he is looking at me;
I, I am happy, I am looking at him.
—Hasteen Klah,
"When They Saw Each Other"

CONTENTS

ACKNOWLEDGMENTS

This book's epigraph is from Hasteen Klah's "When They Saw Each Other," originally published in *Texts of the Navajo Creation Chants*. Ed. Mary C. Wheelwright. Np: Peabody Museum, Harvard University, n.d., n.p. no. 14. Reprinted by permission of the publisher. All rights reserved.

"Arrow Young Men (The Creation of the World)." From Leo J. Frachtenberg. *Coos Texts*. Columbia University Contributions to Anthropology, 1. New York: Columbia University, 1913. 5–14. Reprinted by permission of the publisher. All rights reserved.

"The Chief's Son Who Received the Animal Power." From George A. Dorsey. *The Pawnee: Mythology, Part I.* Carnegie Institute, *Publications* 59 (1906): 312–14. Reprinted by permission of the publisher. All rights reserved.

"The Coyote Called 'Another One.'" From Edward Winslow Gifford. *Western Mono Myths. Journal of American Folk-Lore* 36.142 (Oct.–Dec. 1942): 345–46. Reprinted by permission of the publisher. All rights reserved.

"Destruction of the Kia´nakwe..." From Matilda Coxe Stevenson. *The Zuñi Indians: Their Mythology, Esoteric Fraternities, and Ceremonies.* Smithsonian Institution, Bureau of American Ethnology, *Annual Report* 23 (1901–1902, 1904): 36–39. Reprinted by permission of the publisher. All rights reserved.

"The Eight Young Men Who Became Women." From George A. Dorsey and Alfred L. Kroeber. *Traditions of the Arapaho.* Field Museum, *Anthropological Series* 5 (Oct. 1903): 266–67. Reprinted by permission of the publisher. All rights reserved.

"Falcon Captures the Cannibal Berdache." From A. H. Gayton and Stanley S. Newman. *Yokuts and Western Mono Myths.* Anthropological Records, 5.1. Berkeley: University of California Press, 1940. 34. Reprinted by permission of the publisher. All rights reserved.

"The First Alyha." From A. L. Kroeber. *More Mohave Myths. Anthropological Records* 27 (1972): 17–20. Reprinted by permission of the publisher. All rights reserved.

["The First Hwami"]. From A. L. Kroeber. *More Mohave Myths. Anthropological Records* 27 (1972): 13. Reprinted by permission of the publisher. All rights reserved.

"The Hehe´ya Trick Hüi´ki." From Alexander M. Stephen. *Hopi Tales. Journal of American Folk-Lore* 42.163 (Jan.–Mar. 1929): 34–35. Reprinted by permission of the publisher. All rights reserved.

"The Hermaphrodite." From George A. Dorsey. *The Pawnee: Mythology, Part I.* Carnegie Institute, *Publications* 59 (1906): 138–39. Reprinted by permission of the publisher. All rights reserved.

"The Hopi Ghost Kills and Gambles." From Elsie Clews Parsons. *Tewa Tales.* American Folklore Society, *Memoir* (1928): 28–29. Reprinted by permission of the publisher. All rights reserved.

"How Lizard Sodomized Coyote." From Carobeth Laird. *Mirror and Pattern: George Laird's World of Chemehuevi Mythology.* Banning, CA: Malki Museum Press, 1984. 169. Reprinted by permission of the publisher. All rights reserved.

"Kuloskap and Pukjinskwes." From John Dyneley Prince. *Passamaquoddy Texts.* American Ethnological Society, *Publications* 10 (1921): 22–25. Reprinted by permission of the publisher. All rights reserved.

"Lesbian Love." From Robert H. Lowie. *The Assiniboine.* American Museum of Natural History, *Anthropological Papers* 4, Part 1 (Nov. 1909): 223. Courtesy of the American Museum of Natural History Reprinted by permission of the publisher. All rights reserved.

"Mä'näbus Humbles a Chief's Son." From Alanson Skinner and John V. Satterlee. *Folklore of the Menomini Indians.* American Museum of Natural History, *Anthropological Papers* 13, Part 3 (1915): 303. Courtesy of the American Museum of Natural History. Reprinted by permission of the publisher. All rights reserved.

"Mä'näbus Outwits Turtle." From Alanson Skinner and John V. Satterlee. *Folklore of the Menomini Indians.* American Museum of Natural History, *Anthropological Papers* 13, Part 3 (1915): 263–66. Courtesy of the American Museum of Natural History. Reprinted by permission of the publisher. All rights reserved.

"The Mothway Myth." From Berard Haile. *Love Magic and Butterfly People: The Slim Curly Version of the Ajilee and Mothway Myths.* Ed. Karl W. Luckert. Flagstaff: Museum of Northern Arizona Press, 1978. 82–90. Reprinted by permission of the publisher. All rights reserved.

"Nänabushu Pretends to Be a Woman." From William Jones. *Ojibwa Texts.* American Ethnological Society, *Publications* 7, Part 1 (1917): 139–45. Reprinted by permission of the publisher. All rights reserved.

"Nih'ā^{n}ça^n and the Panther-Young-Man." From George A. Dorsey and Alfred L. Kroeber. *Traditions of the Arapaho.* Field Museum, *Anthropological Series* 5 (Oct. 1903): 96–97. Reprinted by permission of the publisher. All rights reserved.

"Origin Tale." From E. E. Gifford. *The Kamia of Imperial Valley.* Smithsonian Institution, Bureau of American Ethnology, *Bulletin* 97 (1931): 75–81. Reprinted by permission of the publisher. All rights reserved.

"Pleiades and Taurus." From A. H. Gayton and Stanley S. Newman. *Yokuts and Western Mono Myths.* Anthropological Records, 5.1. Berkeley: University of California Press, 1940. 34–35. Reprinted by permission of the publisher. All rights reserved.

"Red-Hair's (Ici´oce's) Hair." From Robert H. Lowie. *Myths and Traditions of the Crow Indians.* American Museum of Natural History, *Anthropological Papers* 25, Part 1 (1918): 141–43. Courtesy of the

American Museum of Natural History. Reprinted by permission of the publisher. All rights reserved.

"Red-Woman and Old-Man-Coyote's Wife." From Robert H. Lowie. *Myths and Traditions of the Crow Indians.* American Museum of Natural History, *Anthropological Papers* 25, Part 1 (1918): 28–30. Courtesy of the American Museum of Natural History. Reprinted by permission of the publisher. All rights reserved.

"The Sioux Woman Who Acted as a Man." From George A. Dorsey and Alfred L. Kroeber. *Traditions of the Arapaho.* Field Museum, *Anthropological Series* 5 (Oct. 1903): 261–62. Reprinted by permission of the publisher. All rights reserved.

"The Story of the Emergence." From Hasteen Klah. *Navajo Creation Myth: Story of the Emergence.* Recorded by Mary C. Wheelwright. Navajo Religion Series, 1. Santa Fe: Museum of Navajo Ceremonial Art, 1942. 39–105. Reprinted by permission of the publisher. All rights reserved.

"Tasinta-Yukikipi." From Stephen Return Riggs. *Dakota Grammar, Texts, and Ethnography.* Department of the Interior, U.S. Geographical and Geological Survey of the Rocky Mountain Region, *Contributions to North American Ethnology* 9 (1893): 121–23. Reprinted by permission of the publisher. All rights reserved.

"The Turtle Brings Ruin Upon Himself." From William Jones. *Fox Texts.* American Ethnological Society, *Publications* 1 (1907): 315–37. Reprinted by permission of the publisher. All rights reserved.

"Two Maidens Who Played the Harlot with Each Other." From William Jones. *Fox Texts.* American Ethnological Society, *Publications* 1 (1907): 153. Reprinted by permission of the publisher. All rights reserved.

"Warrior Girl." From Elsie Clews Parsons. *Tewa Tales.* American Folklore Society, *Memoir* (1928): 191–92. Reprinted by permission of the publisher. All rights reserved.

INTRODUCTION

Several years ago I began to conduct research for an anthology of poetry by gays, lesbians, bisexuals, and transsexuals,[1] and in the process, I accidentally ran across an essay written by anthropologist Will Roscoe that was going to revise my view of the world dramatically. His essay, "Bibliography of Berdache and Alternative Gender Roles Among North American Indians," is the first attempt by a contemporary individual to examine the "berdache" of Native America.[2] *Berdache,* as one learns in Roscoe's essay,[3] is one of many terms used by early European explorers of the North American continent to refer to native gay, lesbian, bisexual, and transgendered persons and a word later adopted by U.S. anthropologists, a borrowing which led to the word's popularity in other disciplines. However, many scholars have recently begun to stop using *berdache* and have substituted "two-spirit" for it.

Roscoe's essay surveys some fifty-seven reports written by anthropologists, historians, explorers, and even medical doctors that have been published since 1500. Each report investigates, in varying degrees, some aspect of the existence of gay and lesbian Native Americans, examining, for example, their daily lives, their place within the tribal societies and tribal faith systems, the native concepts of the origins of the two-spirit, and so forth. Until his groundbreaking work, anthropologists had virtually ignored the two-spirit as a topic of study—except for the handful who had written those brief reports that were buried in old and obscure journals and then discovered and surveyed by Roscoe.

Roscoe's research on the two-spirit was, for the most part, anthropological in focus. My interest in the topic was initially far more general, and very nebulous. When I realized that, among the fifty-seven reports on which Roscoe had based his essay, a number mentioned myths in which two-spirit deities, demigods, or even human beings played a specific or even pivotal role, my interest became more specific. I realized that a literature of gays, lesbians, bisexuals, and transgendered individuals existed in the territory now known as the United States long before the arrival of European colonists; that the literature has been passed from one generation to the next in a manner typical of oral traditions; that the literature is an integral part of—not a deviation from—much Native American culture; and that, although it was likely that much of the literature had been lost as tribes were decimated by conquering Europeans, at least some was still available in sources, principally anthropological studies, not read by—nor even easily accessible to—most contemporary literary scholars. Indeed, what I had stumbled upon was a body of literature heretofore unknown to most students of U.S. literature, and either unknown or ignored by most scholars involved in Native American studies or in gay, lesbian, bisexual, and transgender studies. To ensure that this body of literature would never again be lost, I began searching for the fifty-seven reports to obtain copies of the two-spirit myths. By the end of 1999, I had not only located the myths which Roscoe had identified and indexed in his essay, but I had also uncovered many others. Eventually, I was able to identify and locate over a hundred myths in which at least one two-spirit individual appears.

Typically, the two-spirit individual was a gay, lesbian, bisexual, or transgendered person—in the western definition of gender variance—who often, but not always, adopted the clothing, habits, and/or social roles of the opposite sex. Often they came to realize their alternative gender status when young, and in many cases, this realization was prefaced by dreams or visions. Just as often, a ritual was performed as a rite of passage, to acknowledge publicly the individual's transition from a heterosexual status to the status of two-spirit. While it is easy, and has become acceptable, to think of the two-spirit as the only role available to gay and lesbian Native Americans of the time, the literature on Native America suggests otherwise. While most of the evidence reveals that two-spirits formed sexual relationships with members of their own sex, the same evidence shows that the relationships were not with other two-spirits. Their partnerships were overwhelmingly with individuals who were comfortable in the roles assigned them by virtue of their gender. Thus, a male two-spirit formed a sexual relationship of whatever duration with an individual who was, in terms of his social status, a "heterosexual man"; likewise, a female two-spirit would form a relationship with a "heterosexual woman." When the relationship between a two-spirit and another individual was long-term, male two-spirits were typically considered "wives" of their mates, while female two-spirits were considered their mates' "husbands." For many Native Americans, sexuality seems to have been more fluid than the polarized notion of heterosexuality at one extreme and homosexuality at the opposite extreme allows.

It is of utmost importance to those interested in Native American literature to be aware that the socially recognized role of two-spirit is one aspect shared among most of the Native American tribes, and that its appearance in tribal mythology sanctions the two-spirit role for those tribes. While the anthropologists can tell us how accepted, or not, the two-spirits were in a particular tribe at a particular time, what their duties were, what their daily lives were like, and so forth, it is in the mythologies that we find the "truth" of two-spirit existence. Unlike anthropological studies, myths provide readers with an emotional context for the two-spirit life. Instead of being stripped down to facts and figures as in anthropological reports, the two-spirit's life as depicted in myths speaks to others and interacts with them. In myth, we are offered the drama of a life (even if it *is* a mythological existence)—its highs and lows, its purposes and distractions, its blood and breath. Nevertheless, the myths do not war against the anthropological investigations, but agree with them: For Native America, two-spirit persons have existed since the dawn of time and, in fact, were often at least of equal standing with other members of their tribe, if not more powerful than those in whose midst they existed. The two-spirit myths offer a clarity and a depth to Native American history, social life, and religion that the anthropological literature can only suggest.

The problem one immediately faces while trying to locate any information on the two-spirit is the fact that there is no single word or phrase used in the indexes to the literature which refer to them. As Roscoe's table of "Frequency of English Terms, 1550–1985" reveals ("Bibliography" 155), during the 435 years of written accounts which at least briefly mention the two-spirit, writers employed some fifteen different terms to refer to gay, lesbian, bisexual, and transgendered Native Americans. *Hermaphrodite*, for example, is not only the first term used in the literature, it is also the longest-lasting of them. Although the word *berdache* can be traced back to the latter part of the 1600s, authors did not usually use it until one hundred fifty or so years later. Authors began to use the words *homosexual* and *transvestite* beginning with the early days of the twentieth century. (We must remember that, as the OED reveals, *homosexual,* the first word used which was not inherently derogatory, was not coined until 1892.) Additional terms used by anthropologists, historians, and others include *sodomite, male prostitute, male concubine, boy prostitute, boy concubine, effeminacy, man-woman, half-man, half-woman, woman chief/warrior, man-like woman, Amazon, lesbian, inversion, transsexual, gay, and gender-crosser* ("Bibliography" 154). Given such a wide and varying perception of one concept in the literature, that of two-spirit, it is no wonder that confusion helped to obscure the two-spirit from those researchers who might have shed light on their roles. To make matters even more difficult for the researcher, *berdache* appears in the anthropological literature in nearly a dozen variations from approximately 1673 to 1889: *bardache, berdash, berdashe, Berdêches, bird-ash, birdashes, bowdash, bredache, Broadashe, bundosh,* and *burdash* (*Changing Ones* 174). The word *hermaphrodite* fared only somewhat better in English. Between 1892 and 1953, the variations on *hermaphrodite,* all of which appear in the anthropological investigations, include *Morphy, morphodites, murfidai,* and *morphdites* (*Changing Ones* 175).

The problem is immediately compounded by another important fact: Among Native Americans themselves, the term used for gay, lesbian, bisexual, or transgendered members of their societies differed from tribe to tribe. The Crow, for example, used *boté,* while the Lakota used *winkte.* Complicating an already complex situation is the fact that each Native American term establishing two-spirit status on a member of an individual tribe was often spelled inconsistently, appearing differently in each of one white anthropologist's reports, from one individual anthropologist to another, and from one era or school of anthropology to another. Consequently, in order to conduct comprehensive research on the two-spirit of the Navajo, for example, a researcher must check at least seven different words in the literature—*nutlys, nátli, nu´tle, nádle, nadle, nádleeh, nádleehí*—all of which have been used at various times by various writers to refer to the two-spirit (*Changing Ones* 215). While the root idea of each of these words is consistent in the seven—and that root is the concept of one changing into another[4]—the words themselves are different enough so that a researcher may become easily confused. Complicating matters even further is the fact that, although the Navajo have only one word to refer to both male and female two-spirits, some tribes have several. The Cheyenne, for example, not only differentiated between male and female two-spirits, they also had more words relating to female two-spirits than to their male counterparts. A male two-spirit was *he'eman* and a female two-spirit was *hetaneman*, whereas the phrases *heemanèvo ehazistoz* and *heeo zetaomeaeuowathaazess* referred to sexual acts between lesbians (*Changing Ones* 214). It is not known whether they had a word or phrase to refer to sexual acts between men.

Of the over one hundred existing two-spirit myths, some are as brief as a few sentences, whereas others are many pages in length.[5] In a number of the myths, a two-spirit figure appears only briefly, or the narrator of the myth only alludes to the two-spirit in what we might call an "aside." In many other myths, the two-spirit figure plays *the* principal role in the myth, as in the case of a number of creation myths (such as the Kamia "Origin Tale"), or at least, an important supporting role in the drama that unwinds in the myth. Some of the myths have counterparts in various nations. For example, the Arapaho, Crow, Menomini, Micmac, Nez Percé, Ojibwa, Okanagon, Passamaquoddy, Southern Paiute, and Wappo have at least one myth in which a male figure poses as a woman in order to "marry" another man. In the myths of many tribes, the ultimate trickster figure, Coyote, takes on two-spirit status as, for example, in the Chemehuevi "How Lizard Sodomized Coyote" or the Western Mono "The Coyote Called 'Another One.'"

Many other myths in which two-spirits appear offer explanations, often symbolic but also literal, for events, situations, or landmarks which were an integral part of the day-to-day lives of Native Americans. The Mohave even explain the existence of the male two-spirit in "The First Alyha" and the first female two-spirit in "The First Hwami." For many Native American tribes, myths revealed that two-spirit were decreed to exist by deities or were among the pantheon of gods. For such tribes, then, the origin of the two-spirited individuals, their acceptance within the tribe's social and religious life, and their subsequent roles within the tribe (including specific activities assigned only to them) were sanctioned by divine powers. It is no wonder, then, that two-spirit deities figured often prominently in various types of myths, although most specifically in those depicting the creation of the world or of specific human activities. If tribal gods had sanctioned the two-spirit by either decreeing that two-spirits should exist or, more importantly, if one or more members of the divine pantheon were a two-spirit, human members of the tribe had to accept the two-spirit and his/her role in the society as the will of the deities who ruled over all aspects of their lives, both individual and communal. Thus in response to such divine decree, many tribes created societal roles for the two-spirit which allotted them a significant and respected place in the tribe. It is obvious, then, that many Native Americans were not threatened by gender variance as their European counterparts were (and are), but saw the two-spirits as individuals with special talents which they offered the tribe for its continued existence, its prosperity, and its safety. For those nations with two-spirit deities, the status of two-spirit men and women seems to have often been honored among the communities, including the role of medicine men and women.

The examples of the tribally recognized contributions that two-spirits made to the Native American communities into which they were born are many. Whereas the duties attributed to, for example, the male two-spirit varied from tribe to tribe, generally speaking they took part in men's *and* in women's work as well as engaging themselves with duties unique to their two-spirit role. For some tribes, such as the Crow, a man who decided not to accept the role typically assigned a male could nevertheless contribute to the welfare of the tribe by engaging in valuable work associated with women. Because both male and female roles were valued in many nations, the two-spirit would not be abandoning a higher social status for a lesser one—i.e., in terms of social status, he or she would not be moving vertically, but horizontally; he or she would not be dropping to a *lower* social status but merely moving to a *different* social status. Although most male two-spirits worked at female activities, male two-spirits also joined war parties and engaged in battle—as did female two-spirits. The exploits of the Crow *boté* Osh-Tisch (called, in English, "Finds Them and Kills Them") at the Battle of the Rosebud on 17 June 1876 are legendary.[6] As time progressed, a number of two-spirits found that their roles extended beyond the tribe's territory into the white world. The Zuñi *lhamana* We'wha was not only the toast of the town but also a highly successful delegate between the Zuñis and white societies when anthropologist Matilda Coxe Stevenson hosted We'wha's visit to Washington, D.C., in 1885. It was a successful attempt to foster good public relations between Native America and white America—and between Native Americans and the U.S. government.

For the most part, the two-spirit myths that have been preserved by anthropologists and others belong to nations that lived west of the Mississippi River because, unfortunately, the Native American societies east of it were so badly ravaged by European colonists that, in many cases, their people died out and many of their traditions were lost with them. However, anthropologists were able to study, for example, the Plains societies and to record many, if not most, of their traditions, including their myths. Based on the evidence in the anthropological literature, we can assume that the male two-spirit status was common to a very large number of Native American nations, over one hundred fifty of them, and acknowledgment of and societal sanction for female two-spirit roles existed in at least fifty tribes. Despite such a large evidence for the existence of female two-spirits, most of the extant myths focus on their male counterparts. Unfortunately, only a few myths about the female two-spirit have been recorded and have survived into our time.

Compiling this anthology, I have necessarily been selective, including all those two-spirit myths that are most readily identifiable to contemporary readers as dealing with gay, lesbian, bisexual, and transgendered figures, regardless of the myths' lengths or their tribe of origin. I have also selected those that focus on a two-spirit figure as a prominent, if not main, character of the myth, rather than those in which the two-spirit plays a decidedly peripheral role. In an effort to present a balanced volume that objectively reflects the body of two-spirit myths available, I have included those in which the two-spirit is obviously the antagonist as well as those in which the two-spirit is an instigator of violence.

I have arranged the myths into sections, each section very broadly suggesting the individual myth's purpose: didactic myths, myths of lesbian unions, myths of the origin of the two-spirits, myths of men who became women, origin myths, myths of pregnant men, and myths of violence against two-spirits. I nevertheless realize that any given myth could appear in several of the sections I have created for them—or in others which I am not using. After each myth's title, I have added parenthetically the tribe to which the myth belongs and the date on which it was first published. I have also included the name of the Native Americans who initially told the myths, whom I refer to as "narrators," and to the anthropologists who then recorded them, whom I refer to as "recorders." In some cases, the anthropologists did not include the informants' names in their reports, but only their initials. In such cases, I have included the initials for lack of any other information.

Because anthropologists occasionally printed the myths in large blocks of texts without typical paragraphing, a practice that makes the texts difficult for contemporary readers, I have added paragraph indentations following contemporary practice. I have even done this in some of the myths that do have paragraphs but that have inconsistent or, by contemporary standards, incorrect paragraphing. Some anthropologists also often numbered each sentence in the myths to make pinpointing specific parts of the texts more easy for discussion, I assume, in much the same way as lines in anthologies of poetry aimed at the classroom have numbered lines. In such cases, I have deleted the numbers, again so as not to distract the reader. I have retained all footnotes that appeared with the original versions of the myths, although I have put them at the end of the myth. I have included a few footnotes of my own here and there to clarify points that may otherwise confuse readers.

As important as anything else, the reader must be aware that I see my task in compiling this volume as gathering together materials that have been obscure, many for over a century now, and presenting them to the general reader as well as to scholars—of Native American studies, of gay, lesbian, bisexual, and transgender studies, and of American literature. I would like to believe that this collection will be as important for study as, simply, for enjoyment. I have elected not to interpret the myths, but to allow them to speak for themselves. I would recommend that readers who are interested in the two-spirits and in the interpretations of their lives, societal roles, and so forth, should read the studies by Roscoe, Paula Gunn Allen, and Berniece Medicine that I have listed in the Notes. I would direct those interested in reading more two-spirit-related myths to the bibliography of "Related Myths and Legends for Further Reading" at the end of this volume.

By collecting these texts and arranging them as I have, I have attempted to locate a literature (and, indeed, a history) that existed long before the European colonization of North America, but which was made invisible by the colonists' decrees. Some of the decrees were explicit while others were implicit. Regardless, the effect of each was to destroy the record of an entire people—the gay, lesbian, bisexual, and transgendered peoples of North America. I mean for this book to help document the existence of two-spirit peoples in a real and substantial way. What is immediately obvious and undeniable is that not only does American literature begin with the oral traditions of Native Americans, the beginning of American literature includes gay and lesbian literature in the form of these and other myths.[7] Consequently, a true course of study of early American literature must now not only include those Native American texts that mirror heterosexual life but also a representative sample of the two-spirit literature. To do otherwise would be to perpetuate a lie.

Jim Elledge

Notes

1. The book, *An Architecture of the Invisible,* is forthcoming from Indiana University Press in 2002-3.
2. For this introduction, I have relied on three sources by Will Roscoe, the undeniable expert in the field of gay, lesbian, bisexual, and transgendered Native American studies: "Bibliography of Berdache and Alternative Gender Roles Among North American Indians," *Journal of Homosexuality* 14.3/4 (1987): 81–171; *The Changing Ones: Third and Fourth Genders in Native North America* (New York: St. Martin's, 1998); and *The Zuñi Man-Woman* (Albuquerque: University of New Mexico Press, 1991). Hereafter, I will document all references to these three sources parenthetically within the text, using "Bibliography,"

Changing Ones, and *Zuñi* followed by the page number on which readers may find the information.

Readers will also be interested in, and will gain a great deal of insight from, Paula Gunn Allen's "*Hwame, Koshkalaka,* and the Rest: Lesbians in American Indian Cultures" in *The Sacred Hoop: Recovering the Feminine in American Indian Traditions* (Boston: Beacon, 1986), 245–61 and Beatrice Medicine's "Warrior Women: Sex Role Alternatives for Plains Indian Women," *The Hidden Half: Studies of Plains Indian Women,* ed. Patricia Albers and Beatrice Medicine (Lanham, MD: University Press of America, 1983), 270–74, 278.

3. Since Roscoe began his research into gay, lesbian, bisexual, and transgendered Native America, the word *berdache,* which Roscoe uses nearly exclusively, has fallen into disrepute among some scholars. According to them, it is a derogatory word, and they have convincingly argued for the adoption of "two-spirit" as more pertinent to the Native American view of the gay, lesbian, bisexual, and transgendered individual's existence. I have adopted "two-spirit" throughout this introduction. Readers interested in the debate of *berdache* versus "two-spirit" should see Roscoe's *Changing Ones,* pp. 108–12 and *Two-Spirit People: Native American Gender Identity, Sexuality, and Spirituality,* ed. Sue-Ellen Jacobs, Wesley Thomas, and Sabine Lang (Urbana: University of Illinois Press, 1997).
4. Roscoe translates the Navajo words as meaning "he changes," "being transformed," "that which changes," "one who changes time and again" (*Changing* 215).
5. Others, such as Hasteen Klah's versions of the *Navajo Creation Myth: The Story of the Emergence* and *Hail Chant and Water Chant,* as well as Slim Curly's versions of *Love-Magic and Butterfly People,* have been published as books.
6. In his *Changing Ones* (33), Roscoe reprinted an interesting photograph of Osh-Tisch taken around 1877 or 1878, when Osh-Tisch was approximately twenty-three years old. Osh-Tisch is sitting with a woman who may very well be The Other Magpie, who rode into battle alongside of Osh-Tisch and who was perhaps a female two-spirit.
7. Readers interested in such a view of American literature will find my *An Architecture of the Invisible* of benefit. It will include a number of chant/poems by two-spirited persons, including We'wah and Hasteen Klah, as well as several by anonymous individuals who may or may not have been two-spirited individuals.

Origin of the World

Arrow Young Men (The Creation of the World) (1913)

(Coos)

Recorder: Leo J. Frachtenberg

Two young men were traveling. They stopped in the middle of their journey, (and one of them said,) "How would it be if we two should try it? What do you think about it?"

"It would be good if we two should try it," answered the other one.

"We ought to try it with that soot here."

They had five pieces (disks) of soot. Now they stopped and dropped one piece into the ocean. The world at that time was without land. Everything was covered with water. Again they dropped one piece (disk). The ocean was rolling over the disk.

The next day they dropped another disk. Then they stopped at some small place and dropped another disk into the ocean. They looked at it from above. Now land began to appear, and they saw it. They were very glad when they saw the land coming up.

The next day they dropped another disk. Land began to stick out (come up). They looked frequently at the waves that rolled back and forth continually. "What is your opinion?" said one of the two men. "Shall we try it again?"

"With what shall we try it?" asked the other one. The water was still rolling back and forth.

"Let us split this mat."

They did so, and placed the two pieces over the five disks of soot. Now they went down to examine it. Still the land was not solid enough. So one of them said, "Let us split this basket in two!" They split it, and put it on the sand beach. The waves were held back now, since the water was able to go down through the basket.

Now the young men went down and examined the land. "This will do," said one of them. "It's good that way."

Now they began to look around the world which they had created. There were no trees. "Suppose we set up some trees," said one of them.

"It would be very good," answered the other one.

Then they stuck into the ground the feathers of an eagle. The feathers began to grow and developed soon into fir trees. "All kinds of trees shall grow," said the older man. All the different kinds of trees commenced to grow.

"Suppose we create animals," said one of the young men. "It won't be good if there shouldn't be any animals. The future generations ought to have animals." (Then they created animals.)

Early in the morning they went to look at the world they had created. Suddenly they saw tracks on the ocean beach. "Whose tracks may these be?" asked one of them.

They followed the tracks, and soon came upon a person sitting (on the top of a snag). "You, indeed, must have made these tracks. Who are you?"

"I am a medicine man," answered the person whose face was painted all over with red paint.

"You have no right to travel here. This is our world. We have made it. Are you surely a medicine man?"

They seized the stranger and killed him. Then they spilled his blood in all directions, and said to him, "You will be nothing. The last generation shall see you."

Then they turned back. Suddenly one of them became pregnant. The child could not come out. "What will become of us? We ought to have wives." None of them had done anything; nevertheless, he became pregnant. The child was all the time trying to come out but could not do it.

So they sent some one to the north and told him, "There is a man living there. He is a good man. Bring him here." Someone went to get him.

They went out in a canoe. To their surprise, there were no waves. So they wished that waves would come. "Five times shall the north wind come and (bring) five breakers." And so it was. They were waiting for the fifth wave. And when this came, they went ashore. (They found the man, and brought him to the pregnant person.)

As soon as he saw the pregnant man, he took out the child. It was a girl. From this girl, all the people took their origin. She caused the people to multiply, and to inhabit the world.

Now the young men continued their journey. They once more examined the world which they had created and found it to be good. Everything began to assume its present appearance.

They both had bows. "How would it be if we should shoot towards the sky?" Indeed, they began to shoot. They looked at their arrows as they were shooting them.

"You too ought to shoot one arrow," said one of the young men. "Shoot it so that it shall hit the shaft of mine, and it will look as if it were one arrow; but don't shoot too hard!"

He shot and hit it.

"Shoot again!"

Their arrows became joined and reached down to the place where they were standing.

"Suppose we climb up now!"

"All right!"

They shook the arrows. "Are they firm? Won't they come apart? Now you try to climb up!"

He climbed up. "This is very good indeed."

Then the other man climbed up. They looked down and saw the beautiful appearance of the world which they had created.

Nobody knows what became of the two young men.

Here the story ends.

Origin Tale (1931)

(Kamia)

Narrator: Narpai

Recorder: E.W. Gifford

The earth (pakamat) and the sky lay close together when they were made in the beginning of the world.[1] Between them were the five beings, Chiyuk, Chiyi, Pukumat, Mastamho, and White Woman. Pukumat was the chief god.

Chiyuk and Chiyi reached to the west, where the sky and earth touched, and took handfuls of small red ants (chidasil). These they put on the ground and stirred around with their hands. They did this to make the earth dry, for it was wet. They appointed the god Pukumat to be their son and chief over the people. Mastamho was there as a spirit. He took Pukumat's place when the latter died, as related beyond.

Chiyuk had a brown fox (madkawar) and Chiyi had a red fox (parhau). Chiyi with his fox emerged from the earth first. Chiyuk asked: "How did you emerge?"

Chiyi replied: "I looked up and opened my eyes as I came out of the earth."

As Chiyuk came up with his eyes open, Chiyi picked up earth and threw it in his brother's eyes, blinding him.

Chiyuk and Chiyi made the different sorts of birds, but because of his blindness Chiyuk could not make perfect birds. The mouths and feet were too big. The two brothers put green leaves in the water which sick birds drank and they became well. After making all the birds in the world they reported to Pukumat, who said, "All right."

Chiyuk went hunting and returned home to find that Chiyi had exchanged the foxes while he was away. In anger Chiyuk went into the ground. He wanted to wreck all of this earth and to make all of the birds sick. Chiyi was left alone on the surface of the earth. He discovered the cause of the trouble and braced the earth with his hand, but diseases came up between his fingers.

Chiyuk stayed underground a month and then came up from the east. After a month he disappeared beneath the earth again. He continues to do this even now, spending a month beneath the earth and then a month above it. Above the earth he now appears as the constellation Chiyuk.

Chiyi made all the different mammals, birds, reptiles, fishes, etc., who were in human form at first, but not man. He gave them to Pukumat. At night Pukumat made a fire, so that all the people came to it. Moon attended the meeting also.

Moon said: "I want to get up and tell you about myself. One of the things I wish to tell you is that I desire to go along with the sun, but I want to die in the east. Then after four days I will be reborn in the west. I wanted to tell you this." Then Moon told the people the six month names which they were to use. "These will be my names," he said. The word for month was xasha. This was the sound which the god Pukumat made frequently during his illness, when coughing or clearing his throat.

Then Coyote (xaspa) spoke: "Moon is talking about dying and returning after four days in the west. That is all right."

Moon left for the east, where he became old. Then he went around to the west, where he appeared young. When Moon left, Pukumat was still living. The month of his death is not known.

A little bird (hanuchip) and another little bird (kwasaman) were sitting at the fire. They said: "When a bird dies, he will never return. So it will be with people because, with babies being born right along, there would be too many people."

At this assembly around the fire, there lay on the ground a small lizard (akwatl). He was silent until the sun was rising. Then he talked and immediately he died. Pukumat was with the company, but he said nothing about the dead person. Finally someone arose and asked what to do with the corpse. Pukumat said to take it east. After a few minutes another man asked Pukumat what was to be done with the dead man. Then Pukumat told them to get three poles, lay these over a hole in the ground, and burn the corpse on them. The people did that.

Frog, the daughter of Pukumat, was at the meeting too. She caused her father's death by extracting a hair from his head, putting it in mud, and throwing it to another frog, which swallowed it. That act made Pukumat sick.

Pukumat went to Mount San Jacinto, hoping that Sikapai (the god of that mountain) could cure him. But Sikapai did not know how to cure him, so Pukumat returned. Then he went to a mountain on the California-Lower California border.[2] There the god Sikaiye, whom Pukumat besought to cure him, could do nothing for him.

Pukumat was then taken to WikaaL.[3] He could not be cured there, so he went eastward to the mountain Wiakam, where he died.

When Pukumat died, his blood ran down to the ground and became Mouse (iswaikamayel). Thereafter, Iswaikamayel took Pukumat's place in telling the people in what months to plant and gather crops. The people went to the mountain Wikami, leaving Iswaikamayel behind. He went about stealing food while people were away. He was the first to steal.[4]

Pukumat's body was burned on the mountain Wikami. When the funeral pyre was blazing, it looked as if the mountain were afire. Before the pyre was ignited, the people stood around it. They looked for fire. Coyote suggested that they get fire from the sun. So Coyote went to the sun for fire. Before he returned with it, the pyre was ignited. When Coyote came to the crowd of mourners surrounding the pyre, he leaped over them, seized Pukumat's heart, ran off with it, and ate it. The mountain is covered with grease from the god's heart, and hence called Grease Mountain.

After the funeral, the people assembled at the mountain Wikami.[5] The god Mastamho presided and asked each person if he would be the leader. Donkey arose and said he would be the leader of the people.

Mastamho decreed otherwise, saying: "No; you will carry water and many things on your back."

Donkey replied: "No; I do not want to do that." In a few minutes he lost his human form and became a donkey.

Thereafter, all the people turned into animals. Some grew feathers, some scales, some hair. Then the large birds arose, flew around, and flew back to the starting place. Then all the birds and mammals and other creatures departed, and Mastamho was left alone at Wikami.

Mastamho then created human beings. He made the Yumans first. The following morning he made the Chemehuevi, but he made them pygmies. Then he made the Mission Indians. Clay was the material of which he made men. He made ten of each kind. The pygmies grew into full-sized men.

From the sky, White Woman came to earth at Wikami. She went to the north. Mastamho said to her: "I will give you everything." Others heard this and wished to have everything, too, but Mastamho said they should settle at different places. To White Woman he gave clothing, which he told her not to burn at funerals.

Two white children were first born of White Woman in the beginning of the world. Mastamho said there would be white people in the north. He made European articles, such as coins and steel swords. He threw them all into the river, but said they would come back again. One of these swords (wotat) was picked up by a woman.

White Woman bore many children, all conceived without a man. As these children grew up, they scattered over the world in all directions, especially to the south, where the country became thickly populated. They were short in stature.

After Mastamho had created all the people, he said: "We have nothing here for you to use; we have no pottery."

Hidden under the ocean in the south was the great snake Mayihauchauwit, which had been created by the gods Chiyuk and Chiyi. It was spotted with various colors and was the repository of knowledge.

Mastamho conceived the idea of inviting the great snake to come to the mountain Wikami to attend the mourning (keruuk) ceremony, which the Kamia and other peoples were to hold. He sent a Kamia to invite the monster.

The snake came and entered the keruuk house, but there was room for only half his body. Therefore, they enlarged the house so that he could get his entire body within it. The people who were sitting in the house when the snake arrived had to leave it to make room for him.

Mastamho said: "We should not allow Mayihauchauwit to return to his home. We must burn the house and his body, so that you tribes will get the different songs from his body." Then they burned the house with the monster in it, and the songs issued from his body as spirit persons. Thus, the various tribes got their songs. The Kamia obtained a mourning (keruuk) song cycle, chayautai song cycle, nonyumer song cycle (which the Mohave are said also to have), tomanp song cycle, tomanpkweL song cycle, and tatmayuher song cycle. The last four are said to have issued forth as spirit persons from the second (chayautai). The Cocopa also sing some chayautai songs. Tipai songs were not obtained on this occasion, though they are Kamia songs, sung by both Kamia and Diegueño.

Mastamho now told the people that they should leave the mountain Wikami and go to their future lands. Because they walked in the river water, the tribes became brown skinned. The Mohave settled in the vicinity of the mountain. Some Chemehuevi went a short way to the north, others to the south. The other tribes moved south. Three stopped at Blythe: the Maricopa (Hatpa.inya in Kamia), the Kohuana (Kowan in Kamia), and the Halchidhoma (Halchiyom in Kamia). The other tribes came on south to Yuma, where the Colorado River passes between two bluffs. Some of the Yuma stopped there to take possession of the land in the vicinity. On the hill where the agency buildings now stand, they put up their right hands and said: "We are going to take this land on the north side and the south side." Other Yuma went on to the mountain Wikunyai in Lower California, where they stopped. There they lived many years, planting there a kind of food called hatsot. This was a small orange-colored fruit which grows on shrubs about as tall as a man. After a time, the Yuma moved to Kwasit, where there were big rocks.[6]

Two more tribes came from the north. They followed along the Colorado River and finally stopped at Matkakan (Colonia Lerdo, Lower California). They were the Cocopa and Akwa'ala.

The Kamia came partway with the Yuma, then left them and went to the eastern shore of the Salton Sea.[7] The sea[8] was large then, and where El Centro is now, there was sea. Later they moved to Indian Wells (Xachupai) and to Saxnuwai (near Holtville). There were ten men of each tribe. The ten Kamia men were the ancestors of ten lineages. Some of the Kamia passed through Imperial Valley into the mountains of San Diego County and became the Diegueño. There they had no seeds to plant, but found wild plant foods, deer, and mountain sheep.

The tribes of Mission Indians were also near the[9] southern end of Salton Sea. They became afraid of the Kamia, hence the Cahuilla and other Shoshonean tribes fled northwestward.

Later there came from the mountain Wikami three persons who were to be the Kamia leaders. They were a hermaphrodite[10] called Warharmi[11] and her twin "sons,"[12] both called Madkwahomai. These three had learned much at Wikami. They came south along the Colorado River. They found the feathers of birds which had died, as they traveled along day after day. The feathers were of the birds kak (crow), tokwil, and kusaul. The three travelers made headdresses of these feathers and painted their faces as for war. They brought bows, arrows, and clubs.

From the Colorado River at Yuma, they crossed over to Imperial Valley. Their appearance so frightened the Kamia that they fled in all directions. One Kamia woman did not flee before the three. She was married by one of the Madkwahomai twins. Then the three newcomers and the woman settled at Saxnuwai.

The seeds of maize and beans[13] had been given them by Mastamho. These the three travelers brought from Wikami and planted at Saxnuwai, thus introducing cultivation in the Imperial Valley. Those Diegueño who had gone to the mountains to live failed to receive the seeds. The three travelers brought the seeds of certain wild plants as well.

At Saxnuwai, Warharmi and the twins planted, for they found wet ground there. Before their departure from Wikami, Mastamho had explained how everything was to be done. He had said that Warharmi and the two Madkwahomai were to be farmers and that they should go to dwell among the Kamia, whom Mastamho had sent to live on the shores of the Salton Sea.

The two Madkwahomai had brought bows, arrows, and clubs, which had been unknown to the Kamia hitherto. The twins called a conclave of the Kamia at Saxnuwai and there gave bows and arrows to each lineage and instructed the people in their use. One lineage asked what use the weapons would be, and one of the twins replied that they would need them for war. The Yuma did not receive the bow and arrow. They had been given the feathered stabbing pike (akwil) by Mastamho at Wikami. He said that they would use that weapon in the mourning (keruuk) ceremony and that he would help them make the ceremony. The two Madkwahomai asked the Yuma to bring the akwil and show the Kamia at Saxnuwai.

Thereafter, the different tribes formed alliances and began to fight. The Mission Indians formed one group. In another were the Kamia, Yuma, Mohave, Chemehuevi, and "Apache" (Yavapai). In a third alliance were the Cocopa, Maricopa, and Pima.

The Madkwahomai who married the Kamia woman begot twins. The people were astonished at this dual birth and asked the husband what was wrong. The jealous suspicions of the married brother were aroused against his twin brother. The unmarried brother answered, saying: "You know why you have twins. It is because you are my son. That is why you have boy twins." The husband believed him. Later, twins were born to other women, until the whole Kamia tribe was made up of twins.[14]

Notes

1. The informant was contradictory as to the sex of the parents earth and sky, on one occasion making the first male and the second female, and on another occasion doing the reverse.
2. This is a "cut" mountain, with a pass through it.
3. A little hill in Yuma, where the Southern Pacific roundhouse is now.
4. This mouse is found in logs as well as in the ground.
5. A name cognate with Mohave and Yuma Avikwame; the Kamia locate this south of Fort Mohave.
6. This is on the Mexican side of the international boundary. Yuma lived at Kwasit until gathered on the present reservation. Kadjor, a man living in 1929, once lived at Kwasit.
7. Narpai mentioned old metates plowed up by farmers on the east side of Imperial Valley as evidence of the Kamia having been there.
8. Probably Blake's Sea.
9. Presumably present.
10. Described by the informant as half man, half woman.
11. Cf. Mohave hwami.
12. Not really her sons, Narpai said.
13. The informant Narpai included cowpeas as well as teparies.
14. The lineage of these various people was not known to the informants.

The Story of the Emergence (1942)

(Navaho)

Narrator: Hasteen Klah

Recorder: Mary C. Wheelwright

First World

The story starts in the Running-Pitch place or Jahdokonth. Hashjeshjin, the son of the Fire, whose mother is a Comet, and Etsay-Hasteen, the first man, who is the son of Night and whose father is Nah-doklizh, which is the blue above the place where the Sun has set, were there; also Estsa-assun, who is the first woman, whose mother is the Daybreak and whose father is Nahtsoi which is the yellow light after the Sun has set; also Etsay-hashkeh or Coyote Man, whose mother is Yah-zheh-kih, or the Dawn Light. The fifth who is there is Begochiddy, the blue-eyed and yellow-haired god, the great god, whose mother is a Ray of Sunlight, Shah-bekloth, and whose father is the Daylight, Shun-deen; also Asheen-assun, the Salt Woman, whose mother was Tohe-estan, or Water Woman, and whose father was Tsilth-tsa-assun, or Mountain Man. (He looks like a woman but is a man.) These are the six people who were living on the dark earth or first world, Jahdokonth.

On the dark earth, Begochiddy built in the east a white mountain, in the south a blue mountain, in the west a yellow mountain, and in the north a black mountain, and he also made mountains surrounding all the dark earth and the colored mountains, and these were called Tsilth-nah-n' deel-doi, which means colored mountains which appear and disappear, and in the center of the world Begochiddy made a red mountain.

He also created the red ants, Willachee, and the black ants, Willazhini, which run in a line on the logs in the mountains, and the yellow ants, Willa-klitsoi, and wood ants, Willacheetsai, which are half red and half black, also Nicky-dol-zholi or gray ants. He named them as they were created and smiled as he made them. He also made Nahasan-b' hogahndi, which lives in the ground, and Wolazhi, which is a tiny black ant, also Neho-neh-yahni, or "black bug which flies around," and which is the Midge.

On the east side under the mountains, he planted some bamboo, or Lukatso. On the south side, he planted big sunflowers, N'd'gilly-tso. On the west side under the mountains, he planted Luka, or reed. On the north side under the mountains, he planted small sunflowers, N'd'gilly.

After Begochiddy had created these things, he gave them Tsa-tlai (First Law). In the first world, there was one law; in the second, two laws; in the third, three laws; and in the fourth, four laws.

Begochiddy now created Kay-des-tizhi (Wound in a Rainbow), who is both man and woman. By this time the ants that he had created had increased very much.

Hashjeshjin asked Begochiddy why there should be only one law and why he, Hashjeshjin, should not be able to make some laws. Begochiddy answered: "I made the law, and there shall be no other."

So Hashjeshjin grew angry and said: "Just because you have made the ants and man, you think you are very great and for that reason I will burn the things you have made and the world, too." And four days later Hashjeshjin started burning the world.

Begochiddy told the first man, Etsay-Hasteen, to go to the east mountain and get some earth and some of the Lukatso plants and bring them back to him, and he told Estsa-assun, the first woman, to go to the south mountain and bring him some of the big sunflowers, N'd'gilly-tso, and Etsay-Hasteen also went to the west mountain and brought back earth and Luka (reed plants), and Estsa-assun also went to the north mountain and brought earth and small sunflowers, N'd'gilly.[1]

In the center of the red mountain, Begochiddy stuck the Lukatso, the big bamboo, and all of the creatures that he had created entered into it. The bamboo now started to grow with all that were in it, growing higher and higher until it reached the second world, the blue world, Naho-doklizh-dasakah, overhead, and grew into it. The little tiny black ants came out first into the new world, and after them, the rest of the ants and then the people, and next to the last came Etsay-hashkeh, and last of all Hashjeshjin. When all had climbed out of the bamboo, Begochiddy pulled the bamboo up into the second world, and Hashjeshjin blew into the hole four times which made the hole close up, and the first world burned up and is still burning.

Second World

Begochiddy took the earth brought from the first world and created mountains in the east, south, west, and north, and plants similar to those in the first world, and he planted white cotton in the east, blue cotton in the south, yellow cotton in the west, and black cotton in the north. On this world the soil was not rich enough to plant crops. He created the bumblebee, honeybee, yellow jacket, and the black wasp. He made twin men and twin women, and Begochiddy smiled as he created all these things.

Hashjeshjin did not like this world or the creatures there and told Begochiddy that he wanted to kill the male twins, and Begochiddy answered: "Why not kill both the male and female twins?"

Hashjeshjin answered him twice in the same way and then he killed the twins. So Begochiddy had made two laws.

Then Begochiddy slit the bodies of the male twins from the neck down to the legs, and cut the flesh into small pieces, and cut off the ends of the fingers and toes and put all the pieces back into the heads. He then did the same to the female twins, starting at the feet and cutting upwards, and the pieces he put into their heads as in the male twins. Both the male and female twins were called Ethkay-nah-ashi. He put the Lukatso (bamboo) into the male and female bodies from the head to the legs and he put a small bamboo across the mouths of the male twins, a large sunflower on the right-hand side of the face, a big bamboo across the forehead, and on the left side another sunflower. On the heads of the female twins, he put a reed across the chin and forehead and a small sunflower on each cheek.

Begochiddy then took a piece of bamboo a foot long and put it into the mouth of the male twins and held the other end in his mouth and then he breathed his spirit into the dead male twins and a great sound began in their bodies. And while this sound went on, in the east near the mountains the white cotton began to move, and in the south the blue cotton moved, and in the west the yellow cotton, and in the north the black cotton, and then all the cotton rose and changed into clouds. The white cotton turned into white clouds, the yellow to yellow clouds, the blue to blue clouds, and the black to black clouds. Begochiddy breathed into the bodies of the female twins, and when the great sound began in their bodies, then under the white cloud in the east, grew up Kloh-lachee, the red grass. In the south under the blue cloud, grew the small yellow rabbitbrush, Giss-dil-yessi. In the west under the yellow cloud, grew the Tsay-zhee or gramma grass. And in the north under the black cloud, grew Tohikath, the Water-Bearer. After these clouds and plants were made, the rain began in the east and went around the world in all directions.

When it had rained and the plants had flowered, it made everyone very happy. They went out to the mountains and picked the flowers and smelled of them and wanted to go and live near the mountains so as to be close to the plants, but Begochiddy and Hashjeshjin said: "No, you may go up to the mountains but you must not live there." The people asked this four times and were refused each time.

Hashjeshjin said: "As you are not willing to obey, I will burn the water."

Now Begochiddy created a red mountain, Yoh-lachee, a bad mountain, which gives people sores on their bodies; and he stuck the big bamboo into the top of this mountain and sent Etsay-Hasteen to gather from the east, south, west and north, all the things that had been created. And Etsay-Hasteen brought earth from the mountains and plants and clouds and put them into the big bamboo. Kay-des-tizhi, the man wrapped in the Rainbow, put the Ethkay-nah-ashi under his rainbow robe and they all went into the big bamboo while Hashjeshjin began to burn the water (oil) in the second world.[2]

Third World

The little black ants were the first to come out of the bamboo into the third world which is the yellow world, Nah-klitsoi-dasahkah.

And after all were out of the bamboo, Begochiddy pulled it up into the new world, and Hashjeshjin blew into the hole and closed it up. All the plants, mountains, and clouds that were in the second world were planted in the third world, and Begochiddy created a mountain in the center of this world called Tsilth-tla-del-tai. And he made another mountain Tsilth-n'del-tai, the second mountain, and Tsilth-tah-del-tai, the third mountain, and Tsilth-teen-del-tai the fourth mountain. Then he made Tohe-egleen, or Water Meeting Place, and then Tohe-nostleh, or Crossing Waters, and in the middle of these crossing waters he put Sis-tahilth-lachee, or Red Mountain Turtle. One of these streams ran from west to east and one from north to south.[3] In the east part of the Crossing Waters, he placed Tahilth-lachee, a big turtle which was red in color. In the south water, he placed the red thunder, Iknee-lachee. In the west water, he placed Tabasteen-lachee, red otter, and in the north water, Teoltsodi-lachee, red water monster. Begochiddy then made a quick-sandy spring called Nahodoh-othle, and a place called Lukatso-sakah, meaning the Growing Place of bamboo. Then Begochiddy made Tsilth-lakai, White Mountain (near Telluride, Colorado), and he placed a white thunder bird on the top of this mountain, and he made four cyclones—black, blue, yellow, and white—and hail of four colors and put them inside of the White Mountain. He took the bamboo, and breathed into the Ethkay-nah-ashi, and life came into the mountains, water, and animals that he had created.

Hashjeshjin created the crow, Gahgi, and the magpie, Ea-ah-ee. And Begochiddy made the hummingbird, Data-tehe, and the turtle-dove, Hospiddy. And then through the Ethkay-nah-ashi he breathed life into the birds and gave them voices.

He made trees, and he made all kinds of animals, birds, bugs, fishes, worms, and everything. He appointed the wolf and the mountain lion kings of the animals, and the oriole and mockingbird as kings of the birds.

Begochiddy now created the first man, Etsay-Hasleen (Made Now), and Atrahgeh-Hasleen (Center Man), next Adahgeh-Hasleen (Behind Man), next Hlakah-kestrah-Hasleen (Fourth Man). And then he made four women of the same names. Kay-des-tizhi, Wound-in-a-Rainbow, took charge of all created animals, birds, and human beings, which were all created pairs. Begochiddy now created corn of four varieties: black, white, blue, and yellow. Then he took the bamboo and breathed through the Ethkay-nah-ashi and gave life to all that he had created. And all created life had one language which all spoke and understood. There was no Sun or Moon in this world but the mountains gave plenty of light.

Begochiddy now made himself a Rainbow house, and he and the five gods of the first world were all living under the east mountain, while the people and animals were living together in the middle of the world. The Navajos were there from the beginning, and Begochiddy now made the Hopis and the Zunis. The males were made first and the females afterwards, and he made for the Zunis four gods: one, the tall god called Yeh-nez, and the other three gods called Yehs. He made the Taos (Toh-wulth) Indians and gave them a male bamboo which they had to watch over and gave the Hopi a female bamboo which they were to guard.

The six gods living under the east mountain wanted the Hopis and Navajos to be friends, so they gave a female Ethkay-nah-ashi to the Hopis and a male to the Navajos. By now all the Indians living together made a large group, and Begochiddy was chief of them all, and Etsay-hashkeh, Coyote Man, watched over the Indians and told the six gods how the people were getting on.

The Indians now planted four kinds of corn, and Estsan-natah, Head Woman, told them what to do, and how to grind corn. By this time, they had different kinds of dresses, some white and some striped with colors, and shoes made of white deer hide. They began to grow tobacco, beans, pumpkins, squash; and they planted Bezh-l'entklizi, a red flower which they needed for their eagle ceremony. All the Indians worked together in harmony. They killed the animals, mostly deer, for meat.

Now the first marriage took place, Etsay-Hasleen with Eekai-etahdeh, who was the daughter of Estsan-nahtah, Head Woman. Eekai-etahdeh liked to go down to the river and sit there most of the day. Her husband had the post of Chief-in-the-Morning and told the people when to go hunting and before each hunt called a meeting in his Rainbow Hogahn and gave them tobacco to smoke. The door of this hogahn was made of woven reeds and was a very fine door. Etsay-Hasleen went hunting four days in succession, and each day after he had departed, Eekai-etahdeh went to the river. When Etsay-Hasleen came back at night he found his supper not ready and his wife not there. This made Etsay-Hasleen very angry, and he became jealous. On the fourth day, he slipped away from his men, instead of going hunting, and went down to the river and hid in the bushes where he could watch his wife. (Begochiddy and Hashjeshjin had sent a spirit to appear before the girl and make love to her, but she knew nothing of this.) As Etsay-Hasleen was watching, he saw something swimming towards his wife. It looked like a big bunch of weeds, but as it neared the girl, the husband saw it was a handsome young man, Sethkinh. Though he looked like a man, he was really the Water Horse, Kahilth-klee, and he had put a lot of weeds on his head to conceal him in swimming. The young man and the girl talked a while, and the husband became very jealous and went home into his Rainbow house and laid down thinking of his wife, and he did not even smoke.

When the girl thought it time for her husband to have returned from the hunt, she went home and found him there and said to him: "When did you get back from the hunt?" and he did not answer. She asked him four times with no answer, and she then cooked some supper and served it in a very finely made basket. She was angry at his not answering her question and she told him so.

The husband then said: "I am angry, too, at the way you have behaved," and pushed the food away with his foot. So his wife understood that he knew what she had been doing and she got up and ran off to her mother. She told her mother everything, and that her husband was angry with her, and her mother grew very angry and said: "Your husband is not supporting you properly although he has plenty of meat and corn and is rich." The mother ran over to the Rainbow Hogahn and sat down outside the door. And while she sat there, she scolded her son-in-law very harshly and then she went back to her own home.[4]

Etsay-Hasleen did not answer her, but got up and went to another hogahn which belonged to Kay-des-tizhi who was rich and had plenty of food and things. Etsay-Hasleen called the three other chiefs together and made them a speech, telling them about his wife and his mother-in-law, and saying that he thought they should all resign from being chiefs as they could not keep order, and they decided to do as he said.

Begochiddy knew all about this trouble, and he and the five gods came to Kay-des-tizhi's hogahn and called the head people and the chiefs of the birds and animals to come to a Council. So they all came and went into the hogahn, and Begochiddy said to them: "I am going to separate the men and the women, and the female birds and animals. All the males are to go and live across the river, and the females are to stay on this side of the river." After this speech they agreed that this was right and should be done.[5]

The chiefs told their people about this, and they said that they would do as Begochiddy had ordered. Kay-des-tizhi was to lead the men across the river and also take charge of the corn-grinding stones. So four big boats were made from a tree called Nash-konh and they named the boats Nash-konh after the tree. Kay-des-tizhi took all his goods and property and all of the male children and loaded them into one boat, and Begochiddy watched and saw that all the males crossed over the river. All went except a young Blue Fox man and a young Yellow Fox man, Mah-ih-doklizhi-sethkinh (Blue Fox Handsome Man) and Mah-ih-klitsoji-sethkinh (Yellow Fox Handsome Man). Both had flutes, and at night while the women were grinding corn, they played their flutes to them. The flutes were made of small bamboo, and when the women heard them, they laughed and had a merry time. Begochiddy soon found out that he had overlooked the two Foxes, and he made them go across the river to the rest of the males.

The men were strong and well-fed as they had plenty of corn and beans, and tobacco; and they made farms; and Kay-des-tizhi was their cook. The women also planted corn and beans, but the harvest was very poor; the corn was scanty and wormy; and their clothing was wearing out as they had no new skins to make new clothing. Estsan-natah, Head Woman, came up to Begochiddy and begged him to let them go back to the men as the women were very poor and hungry and were tired of living alone. Begochiddy said: "Very well, all is forgiven; go back to your men, but I make for you this third law: 'The male shall rule and whatever your chiefs say, that must be done.'"

They all agreed to this, and then Begochiddy said: "If any other evil thing happens, I will make a flood to destroy you."

The women all said: "Very well, we will keep the home clean, cook the food, and care for the children."

So the females were all taken across to the males, and they started to make new clothes of cotton and deerskins of which the men had plenty. The men had plenty of food, meat, and corn, but they did not have any beads.

One day Estsa-assun and Asheen-assun went walking by the Water-Crossing-Place, or whirlpool, called Away-nah-olth, and there they saw a baby floating in the middle of the whirlpool. They went and told the gods about the baby, which had long black hair. Etsay-hashkeh, after hearing this from the women, said to himself: "I think I will go and see this baby," and he went towards the whirlpool from the east, then from the other three directions, south, west, and north, and each time he saw the baby floating. When he came from the fourth direction, he lifted the baby out of the water and hid him under his white robe, which was called Mah-ih-jilthli-lakai, and he kept the baby hidden inside of his robe for four days.

Four days after the baby had been stolen, a great noise began to sound in the east, south, west, and north. And though Begochiddy knew what this meant, he told a crow to go to the east to see what was the matter, and the crow came back and said a storm was coming. To the south he sent a magpie, who saw a big blue storm coming. To the west he sent a hummingbird, who saw a yellow storm coming. To the north he sent a dove, who found a white storm there. And the six gods went in all four directions gathering the plants, animals, and everything that had so far been created. They placed them in Lukatso, the big bamboo.

Estsan-natah, Head Woman, said to her son-in-law, Etsay-Hasleen: "I know many prayers and you know many songs to protect us." And she said to him also: "From now on, all the people who have been good and kind will go up to the fourth world, but all the bad people will go down to the first world, or Burning-Pitch-Place."

Meanwhile, big storms were approaching from the four directions, and Begochiddy told Estsan-natah to sing her songs to protect the people. From this origin, come the three first ceremonies. One ceremony is the story of the Ethkaynah-ashi; another the prayer and song; and another the song only. But no ceremony was held at the time of the creation. The songs and prayers used at that time are still used in the ceremonies. If people are bad and know this ceremony and ask for forgiveness, they need not go to the burning world. If a man kills another and repents and knows the ceremony he need not go down to the lower world, and the name of the ceremony is Chalth-yilth-nahgih-eh, or Wanderer-in-the-Dark. It can be held for sickness, when the sickness results from crime. The spirit of the Ethkaynah-ashi is the spirit of life and also is the spirit of the Wanderer-in-the-Dark.

There were two spirits who did not go up to the fourth world, one male and one female. The female was named Kith-nah-ha-klithy, which is the Spirit of Dusk which works with the Spirit of Darkness who is the male spirit, Kith-nah-kliz-hini. The female spirit lived in the house of red fire, Konth-lachee, with a door made of smooth wind, Niltche-dil-kohni. The male spirit lived in the House of Darkness, Chalth-yilth-hogahn, with a door named Nchochee-dothinlah.

Now the hot waters named Toh-bazdezkih and Toh-bazdeznah were rushing upon Lukatso (bamboo) and all the creatures and plants hurried to get into it. But it would not start to grow, so they moved it to Tohe-egleen, where the waters meet, but it would not grow there, so they moved it again to Nah-hodoh-othle, Quicksand Spring, where it began to grow at once. The Turkey People did not get into the bamboo but clung outside to its joints, and, as the waters rose, their tail feathers dipped into the white foam, which has made their tail feathers white on the ends to this day. As the water rose, they would climb up to the next joint until the water rose to it, and then they would climb up to another joint. The Lukatso kept growing until it could grow no more, and still it was not high enough to reach the next world, so Begochiddy made a white cloud above it and the people climbed up to it while the Spider Woman and the Spider Man wove a web around the edge to prevent the people from falling off.

Begochiddy saw that the chiefs and people were excited, so he called a Council to see what they could suggest about how to reach the upper world. The wolf chief had a white cornstalk in his hand and was dressed in the white tail feathers of the eagle. The lion chief had yellow corn in his hand and was dressed in the yellow tail feathers of the eagle. The lion and wolf knew that someone had done wrong to bring about such danger from the waters and asked their people who had sinned, and the people accused the chiefs because they said that they themselves had done nothing wrong. Begochiddy told the lion and the wolf that because they did not please the people they could not be chiefs any longer. And so the mockingbird and hummingbird chiefs were the only ones left to govern, and they tried to find out who had done wrong but could not succeed.

Begochiddy knew the sinner and also knew the people's thoughts.

Among those at the Council was the chief of the locusts who wore an arrow on his forehead made of an eagle tail. He asked Begochiddy why he had called the Council, and Begochiddy answered: "The people are afraid of the waters and do not know how to get into the upper world."

The Locust said: "I know how to reach there. Call the Ant People who are living at Nehochee."

So the Ant People were asked to try to dig a hole through to the upper world (this is called the Black Trail), but they could not succeed. And the yellow ants then tried, but they had to give it up (this is called the Yellow Trail). Meanwhile, the Turkey People were making noises because their tails were still dipping in the water as they clung to the outside of the bamboo. Begochiddy asked the tiny black ants if they could dig through to the upper world (their road is called the Sparkling Trail), but they could not. So Begochiddy said to the locust chief: "Sechai (Grandfather), please show us how to reach the next world." And the Locust put his arrow on his forehead and shot up into the next world. He had great powers.

Fourth World

The Locust came up through the crust and then through mud and water, for water covered the whole fourth world, and over it was flying a great white bird, Cheestehi-lakai. He had arrows with him, and when he saw the Locust, he flew at him to kill him, but the Locust splashed water about, and the bird could not find him. The great bird asked the Locust: "Where did you come from, and who are you?" To show the Locust his power, he took his arrow and swallowed it and then drew it out again, and asked the Locust if he could do anything like that, for if he could it would prove that he was great and powerful and could live on the fourth world.

The Locust had now come to the top of the water and was floating on it, resting with crossed legs. He answered the great bird: "Yes, I can do that. Watch me!" And he thrust his arrow through his heart and drew it out again, saying to the bird: "Can you do that? I have more power than you." So the bird was frightened and flew off to the east, and was not seen again.

From the south now came a big blue bird who tested the power of the Locust by thrusting his arrow twice down his throat; and the Locust conquered him by thrusting his arrow twice through his heart, and the blue bird flew back to the south.

A great yellow bird came from the west who swallowed his arrow three times, and the Locust thrust his arrow through his heart three times, and the yellow bird flew west again.

From the north came a white bird, and thrust his arrow down his throat four times, then the Locust thrust his arrow through his heart four times, and the bird flew north again. So the Locust won the contest of power with the great birds in this world.

Meanwhile, the people still in the bamboo were very nervous because it was waving about in the air, and they did not know what was happening to the Locust. When he came back by the hole to the lower world and began to speak to the people in the bamboo, his voice made a chee-chee sound because of the hole through which he had thrust his arrow. He told them that he had had a hard time getting up into the upper world, and he told them about the water, and of his trial of strength with the big birds, and he called the people his grandchildren.

Begochiddy asked all the chiefs and captains of the people: "Who will go up to the fourth world?" But no one would go, so Begochiddy went himself, and when he reached the upper world, he came out on a big pile of mud in the middle of the water.

To the east he saw a great white cloud, and he made a Rainbow Lightning which carried him to this cloud. And when he reached it, he found there Hashje-altye, the great god of the Yeh-bechai, and Hashje-altye was glad to see him and said: "How are you, my grandson? I own this world and have great power. The big birds tried to claim this world, but I have conquered them, and they are my servants." They were very happy together and then Begochiddy went back running on the water to the pile of mud at the center of the world.

Then he saw a blue cloud to the south with showers dropping from it, and he went there on the Rainbow and found Beganaskiddy, Bringer of Seeds, who welcomed Begochiddy, and they were happy together. Beganaskiddy greeted Begochiddy as Hashje-altye had done, and afterwards, Begochiddy ran back on the water to the center of the world.

Then seeing a yellow cloud in the west, he went there on the Rainbow and found Hashje-hogahn, and they had the same intercourse as Begochiddy had had with the other gods, and then he went back to the center of the world running on the water.

To the north there was a white cloud, raining, and Begochiddy went there on the Rainbow, and found another Beganaskiddy. The same ceremony took place, and then he came back to the center of the world again.

Meanwhile, Lukatso, the bamboo, was still swaying about, and the people inside of it were very much worried.

Begochiddy stood on the pile of mud at the world's center and saw Hashje-altye, the two Beganaskiddy, and Hashje-hogahn standing up to their breasts in the water at the east, south, west, and north of the world. And Begochiddy waved his hand to each god in turn, and they rose as he greeted them onto the surface of the water. Then Hashje-altye took his cane and pushed the water back slowly to the east, and Beganaskiddy pushed harder to the south, Hashje-hogahn pushed harder still to the west, and Beganaskiddy at the north pushed very hard so that the earth shook from the blow, and all the water ran off in different directions and made rivers. There was nothing where the water had lain but petrified wood and mud badlands, but there was water all around the earth, and that was the ocean. Where the water had lain, there were beasts who had been living in the water, but when Begochiddy blew on them, they turned into strange shaped rocks, and as he continued to blow, a crust formed on the mud. He looked to the east and saw figures away off, and he went towards them and found them to be gods: Yeh, with blue faces; Hashje-baka, male, and Hashje-baahd, female; six males and six females. In the south there were the same gods, in the west the same, and in the north the same, and they were beautiful.

Begochiddy went back to the Lukatso, bamboo, and found the people much excited, and they were very glad to see Begochiddy, and when he came back to them they called him Sechai (Grandfather). He told them that he had met many people above and that the world was good. They were very glad to hear that, and then Begochiddy sent Badger up to see the world. When he reached the hole, he tried to jump onto the crust, but he broke through, and that is the reason why his paws are black to this day.

Begochiddy asked how the wet earth could be dried, and they sent up to the fourth world white thunder (Iknee-lakai) from the white mountain, also white cyclone (Niholtso-lakai) and white hail (N'dlohe-lakai), and black, blue, and yellow cyclones. When the hail and thunder and cyclones hit the petrified wood and the mud columns which stuck up out of the mud, they were broken into pieces. Then the cyclones blew until they had dried the mud. And they sent five dust devils, Nastoldisse, to trim up the rock pillars and make holes in them. After that, five little whirlwinds were sent up, and they spread the tiny stones about smoothly.

Then the storms all went below to the third world from which they came, and the Lukatso began to grow again. And the people came up into this world led by the ants, with the turkey people coming last. Begochiddy pulled the bamboo up by the tassel on top and then threw the tassel back into the hole, which is why Lukatso, the bamboo, has no tassel now. This fourth world they called Hahjeenah.

The water from the third world came up into the hole after the people, and Begochiddy saw it and asked: "What is the reason that the Water keeps coming up?" He blew and blew into the hole but could not stop it, and they were afraid it would overflow into this world.

So the chief men held a council, and Etsay-Hasteen and all of them were very much worried and frightened, and each asked the other: "Who has done wrong and caused all this trouble?"

Begochiddy said: "If none of you know who has done wrong, I think it may be Etsay-hash-keh, Coyote, who is the cause of it."

And he went up to Etsay-hash-keh and opened his white robe and showed the baby he had stolen. It had yellow hands and looked very strange. Begochiddy took hold of the baby, but Etsay-hash-keh would not let it go, so Begochiddy dropped it, and Etsay-hash-keh threw the baby into the hole to the lower world, saying: "This is what has been the cause of the trouble."

The baby fell on the forehead of a large water monster which was in the water at the bottom of the hole, and then the monster sank down in the water and took the baby down with it, and after that, the water ceased to rise towards this world and has always remained at that level.

There was nothing to make fire with in this new world, and the people wanted fire but did not know how to get it. The only person who had fire was Hashjeshjin, who kept away from the rest of the people. They saw smoke on the horizon far out, and Etsay-hashkeh, the Coyote, went over to see what it was. He found Hashjeshjin and Dontso (the white-headed fly) lying asleep, and all around them in four directions were river boulders burning like wood. And he stole some of the fire and ran back to the people and gave it to them.

Ceremony of the Sweat House Where Creation of the World Began

Begochiddy then called the people together and said: "Let us make plans as to how we shall live." But no one would plan at all and there were no ideas, so Begochiddy said: "Let us make a sweat house for purification."

"But what shall we build it of?" said the people.

Begochiddy replied: "It is close to where Tchah, the Beaver, lives and we will borrow some material from him." Etsay-Hasleen went and borrowed some sticks from the Beaver and brought back a lot as he had plenty.

The people then said: "There are no rocks here to build with."

Begochiddy said: "There are plenty. Ask Deh-nozzi (the mountain sheep) for some."

So Etsay-Hasleen went and got plenty of stone from the mountain sheep who said: "You are welcome to them."

The people asked: "What shall we have for fire?"

Begochiddy said: "Go to Hasteen Dontso (the fly), and he will give you fire." He gave them fire gladly.

And the people asked: "Where can we get water?"

Begochiddy said: "Tabasteen-etahdeh, daughter of the Otter, will give you water." (They sing first of wood, then of stone on the wood, then of fire under the wood, and afterwards of bathing in the water.) For the roof of the sweat house they placed Rainbows, crossing from four directions to hold it up, and then the Robe of Darkness was placed over the Rainbows. Stones were brought and placed in the middle of the house. (They are now placed on one side of it.)

The people now asked: "What shall we have to cover the door?"

Begochiddy replied: "Go ask Nasjah-hasteen, your grandfather, the Owl, and he will tell you."

The Owl said: "Yes, I have white, blue, yellow, and black colored robes and you may have as many as you wish, and I also have robes that flash." And the people chose a flashing robe and put it over the door, borrowing it from the Owl.

Then they all went into the sweat house except Begochiddy, Hashjeshjin, Etsay-hashkeh, and the women, for women were not allowed in the sweat house. And they sang, and Etsay-Hasteen led the singing. They sang of the fire, the stones, the wood, the water, and the sparkling robe, describing all of these things, and then they sang about the heat.

All the people who had loaned the things to make this sweat house stood about outside; and the great Owl stood on the top of the roof, listening to the songs which described the things used in the sweat house, and also thanked the givers for their help.

When the people came out of the sweat house, Begochiddy told them to rub themselves with earth, which they did, thanking the earth as they did it. Then they went into the sweat house again, and the Locust appeared and said: "I will sing for you." So they all went in together and the Locust sang to them. He sang about what he had done in helping the people to come up into this world, and about the contest with the great birds. Meanwhile the daughter of the Otter brought water in a wooden bowl and left it by the door outside, and when the people came out for the second time, they bathed in this water.

Then they went into the sweat house again and began to plan to build some mountains on the earth. The first was Siss-nah-jini (Holy Mountain of the East), the next was Tsoll-tsilth (Mount Taylor), then Nahtah-has-eh (Mountain south of Zuñi), next Dogo-slee-ed (San Francisco Peaks), then Debeh-entsah (La Plata Mountains), next Tsilth-nah-ot-zithly (Huerfano Mountain), next Johl-een (Pedernal Peak), next Trada-deen (a peak of the Jemez range).

Then they planned some rivers, Toh-bakahni, the male (San Juan) river, and Toh-ba-ad, the female (Rio Grande) water; then a lake, Hahjeenah, where the people came out of the bamboo (near Silverton, Colorado).

Then they planned some more mountains, Tsilth-lakai (White Mountains), Tsilth-kah-del-kah (Chuskai Mountains), Tsilth-il-entai (mountains near Chin Lee, Arizona), Tsilth-ti-del-tai (Sangre de Cristo range near Santa Fe, New Mexico), Tsilth-teen-del-tai (Jemez Mountain), Tsilth-beel-yah (Bill Williams Mountains south of San Francisco Peaks, Arizona). And then going westward towards California they planned these mountains, Tsilth-endes-kai, Tsilth-kislakai, Tsilth-dithklith, Tsilth-klitsoi, Tsilth-en-dokahnt, Tsilth-dogidshegar, Tsilth-binneh-hasteen-tseel, Tsilth-neeteen-tseel, and Tsilthran-es-tseel (Bright Shining or Blue Mountain, on Santa Cruz Island, California).

Then they planned to create the Sun, Johonah-eh, and the Moon, Klayonah-eh, and many stars: the Morning Star, Sontso; the Evening Star, which is also Sontso; the North Star, Sontso-dohn-dohzeedi—The One That Does Not Move; and Sontso-deshyi, the Red Star Overhead. Also they planned the constellations: the Dipper, or Male Stars Going Around like a Clock, Nohokos-bakahni; the little Dipper, or Female Stars Going Around, Nahokos-ba-ahdi; and the Pleiades or Seven Stars which is Dilgeheh. They planned also: Orion, Etsay-etsosi, the Thin Man; the Rabbit's Feet, Gah-atayjih; the Milky Way, Eekai-estahi; the Crown, Nashi-taythli; and Taurus, Bisolai or Two Stars Together; and the Great Snake of the North, Kleeshtso. They also planned Tah-zhuni, Smoky Star or Nebula; Dont-whutso, Two Stars Hooked Together; Sont-bidai, the Star with Horns; also Sont-eh-dekah, a Star Out of Sight in the East; and the Coyote Star, also in the east, called Mah-ih-besont. And all of these stars, mountains, the Sun, Moon, and the rivers were planned while the people were in the sweat house.

Then they began to plan the months. Each month had its own name and character and some of them had their own stars. The star for November was Hasteen-sikai (Old Man Bending Over); and this was called Niltche-tsosi, the Small Wind Month. The December star is Azay-tso (First Big Medicine), and it was called Niltche-tsoi, or Big, Cold-Wind Month. The January stars are Gah-atay-ih (Rabbit Tracks or Rattle), and this month was called Zus-entlis, or Thin, Icy Sheet. The February stars are Eekai-estahi (the Milky Way), and it was called Atsah-beyazh, or Young Eagle Month. March's name is Wooz-cheed (Noise Made by Eaglets), and it was called Iknee-tsosi or Little Thunder Month. April was called Tahn-chill (Small Growth), and the Canyon Wren belongs to that month, and its stars are Tuzhibegay (Turkey Tracks). Another name for April is Sah-tah-debeh, meaning Mountain-Sheep-Have-Lambs month, and a bird called Debeh-neh (Phoebe) also belongs to it. May was called Tahn-tso (Large Growth), and its star is Datsahni (Porcupine). June's name was Ayah-zush-chilly, meaning Early-Greens-Are-Grown. Its star is Kleeshtso, or the Great Snake. July was called Ayah-zush-tso, meaning Large Growth and Young Fawns month, and Wuzzy-gishi, the measuring worm, belongs to it. August's name was Binni-tahn-tsosi, meaning Corn-Tassels-Have-Come, and the Anlthtahni, or Corn Bugs, belong to it. Its stars are all the small stars in the center of the sky. September was named Binni-tahn-tso, meaning When-Everything-Is-Ripe, and Even-the-Mountains-Are-Ripe. Its stars are Nahshalth-helee (the Ducks). October was called Gahnji, meaning Half-Winter-and-Half-Summer, and its star is Sontso-dohn-doh-zeedi, meaning North-Star-Stands-There.

These things they planned to make upon this world. And then they came out of the sweat house and made another Hogahn of Rainbows called Hodayah which belonged to Kay-des-tizhi, the Man-Wrapped-in-a-Rainbow. And inside the Hogahn they spread many kinds of robes, and all six of the gods and all the Yeh gods and all the chiefs gathered in this Hogahn for a big Council.

And they sang the "Beginning of the World" song: "Nahteen Odolith."

...

The spirits of all the things about to be created were also in the Hogahn with the gods and the chiefs. All the corn and all the seeds were brought by the Yeh gods at Begochiddy's request. Hashjeshjin brought all the stars, the Sun, the Moon, and all the Light, and the other people brought the rest of the things that were to be on this world. They were all in the Hogahn.

They decided to place the mountain Siss-nah-jini in the east. And they made a pile of dirt to represent it in the Hogahn. And they made the spirit for this mountain. And then all the mountains that have been named before in this story were placed in their proper positions in the Hogahn. They put the Sun in the east and the Moon in the west; and in the middle, they placed the Chuskai Mountains and Black Mountain, which is near Chin Lee, and also the Jemez Mountains. And they made a song about the creating of the mountains. And they made spirits like men and put them into all these mountains and into the Sun and the Moon.

Then they sang the song of the Holy Spirit of Darkness.

...

While they were creating the spirits, they always sang.

Hashjeshjin and Choostaigi, who are the black gods and are brothers, now put their own spirits into the stars and the mountains, and these spirits were in human form in the likenesses of Hashjeshjin and Choostaigi. Then Begochiddy told the Council that all of the songs which had been sung since the making of the first world should be remembered by men forever and that also they must remember all the names of the mountains. And all the other gods repeated what he had said.

Etsay-Hasteen, the first male, and Estsa-assun, the first female, who have the spirit of sickness and give it to men if they do wrong, said to the people: "If you do not remember these things and reverence them, we will bring sickness upon you."

And all the gods said the same. And the Yeh gods were appointed to watch over the people, and they gave flint to them so that they could get fire.

Begochiddy said: "We must hurry and create the Spirit-of-the-Earth, Nahastsan-be-esteen, which is the Spirit that makes things grow."

So they created this Spirit, who was painted with a yellow stripe across her mouth, a blue stripe across her nose, and on her eyes a black stripe and on her forehead a white stripe, and she had blue horns with black tips. The Spirit had eagle feathers on her head, and on the feathers were different kinds of birds, and in her hand she had a pollen basket, and she was wrapped in a blanket made of everything that grows on the earth.

Then they created the Spirit of the Sky, Yaah-dithklithy-be-esteen, the Rain and Cloud Spirit, who was dressed like the Earth Spirit except that he had black horns with blue at the ends. He had a headdress of clouds and on the clouds were all kinds of rain and fog. And in his hand he carried a water jug, and he was wrapped in a black cloud robe. He controls the rain.

The Earth and Sky Spirits are connected with corn pollen. Their hands and feet are clasped together, and the mouth of one of these Spirits is connected with the other. And also they have a black wind and a blue wind which work together and this is called Tradadeen-yeh-kaneh-de-azh. (There is a prayer about this which is part of the ceremony). Sahanahray and Bikay-hozhon are the Holy Spirits to the Earth and to the Sky.

They decided that the spirit of Siss-nah-jini, the Holy Mountain of the East, should be dressed in white shell beads, but the spirit of Tsoll-Tsilth (Mount Taylor) became jealous because he wanted to wear white shell, and they argued with him four times about it. Finally it was decided that Siss-nah-jini's spirit should be dressed in white shell with a big white shell for a headdress. And they gave him the white corn to carry. And his blanket was made of morning light. And they put a small white shell in his mouth.

Tsoll-tsith's spirit was dressed in turquoise in the same way as Siss-nah-jini's, but his blanket was turquoise, and they gave him bluebirds, and they put turquoise in his mouth.

The spirit of Dogo-slee-ed (San Francisco Mountain) was dressed in abalone shell. They gave him yellow corn to carry, and his blanket was made of yellow sunset light, and in his mouth was put a small abalone shell.

The spirit of Debeh-entsah (La Plata Mountains) was dressed in jet. His blanket was a robe of night blackness, and he was given all the game, deer, sheep, antelope. And in his mouth was put jet.

The spirit of Tsilth-nah-ot-zithly (Huerfano Mountain) was dressed in all kinds of colored clothing, and they gave him a robe of agate and put in his mouth white crystals.

The spirit of Johl-een (Pedernal Mountain) was dressed in all kinds of jewelry, and his blanket was made of rainbows, and they put corn pollen in his mouth.

There are two mountains which are built like men, the Chuskai Mountains and the Black Mountains. Niltsa-tseel, the Rainy Mountains (Chuskai range), was dressed in Natseen-nahi. His head is Beautiful Mountain. He has a turquoise rattle. His hand is a mountain near Lukachukai, his feet are two peaks west of Tohatchi, and the red patch of earth at Toadalena is his heart. The spirit of Tsilth-klizhin, or Black Mountain, which is near Chin Lee, is dressed the same as the Chuskai Mountains, in Natseen-nahi. His feet are near

Indian Wells, his tail is close to the Ganado, the trail to Oraibi is his middle, and in the center of Black Mountain is a hollow space where his ribs are. His heart is in the Black Mountains and his head is north near the San Juan River. His hands are the cliffs northwest of his head, near Marsh Pass, and he had a big ear of corn in his hand, Tsakahn.

The mountains that they had built in the first world were now remade in this fourth world, and the Jemez and Sangre de Cristo Mountains were both dressed in turquoise. Santa Fe Mountain is called Tradadeen-tsilth (Corn Pollen Mountain), and Jemez Mountain is called Anlthtahni-tsilth (Corn Bug Mountain).

The Coyote now said: "Give me some dirt out of which you are making mountains!"

But they refused, saying: "You are not clever enough to make mountains."

He said: "Yes, I am clever enough."

He asked this four times, and finally the gods gave him some of the earth which was left after making so many kinds of mountains, and the Coyote took it and made a peak in the south and decorated it with aloe. He said: "This will be called my mountain." It took the shape of his paws and it has that shape now, and is called Pagosa Peak.

Then they made the Sun of fire with a rainbow around it, and they put the Turquoise Man into the Sun as its spirit. (The Sun should be represented with woodpecker feathers around it and with horns.) The Moon was made of ice with a rainbow around it, and the spirit of the Moon was the White-Shell-Man. (The Moon should be represented with horns also.)

Then they made a black wind, and they put the spirit of the Abalone Man into it. This is the east wind. They then made a yellow wind and put the spirit of the Red Shell Man into it. The winds also have horns, and wear twisted wind robes around them. Then they made the Fall and Winter and put them in the north and west; and they made the Spring and Summer, and placed them in the south and east, each to be six months long. The Coyote claimed one month which was October, and Begochiddy made a prayer stick of Lukatso (bamboo), half yellow and half white, representing summer and winter, and gave it to him in answer to his claim. October is the mixed-up, or changing, month and is so known to all the Indians.

Then all the spirits which had been made went into the places where they belonged, and they raised the Sun and Moon and Stars and Winds and placed them in their proper places. They were all spirits. Hashjeshjin placed the North Star and said that everything was complete and that he was glad. Begochiddy said to Etsay-Hasteen: "Why do you not place some stars?" So Etsay-Hasteen made the Big Dipper and placed it, and dressed it in feathers, and gave it horns. And Estsa-assun also took stars and placed the Little Dipper. And Etsay-Hasteen also placed the Seven Stars. (Hashjeshjin claimed that the Seven Stars were on his foot, and on his knees and hips and back and shoulders, and on the side of his face.) Estsa-assun picked up another star, Etsay-etsosi, and placed it at the south. She also picked up another star, Etsay-etso, and placed it. And she placed the Milky Way and the Crown and the Porcupine Star, and the Southern Cross. Etsay-Hasteen arranged the Rabbit's Track and placed the Porcupine Star and the Horned Star and several others. They took turns in placing the stars.

Then Etsay-hashkeh, the Coyote, said: "Let me try," and he asked for two stars. So they gave him two, but he could not find a good place in which to place them, and had to put them close together, and called them the Fighting Stars. Then he asked them for another star and he placed it at the south near the horizon (Antares), and called it the Coyote Star. It goes to sleep after the Sun sets. He was still greedy and asked for more but was refused, so he filled both paws full of stars and threw them into the sky which made the tiny stars which cover it all over. Hashjeshjin's is the Comet Star with a tail.

Then they placed twelve big white cyclones (Niholtso) in the east under the edge of the world, and twelve blue cyclones (Niholtso-doklizh), under the edge of the world at the south, and twelve yellow cyclones (Niholtso-klitsoi) in the west under the edge of the world, and twelve black cyclones under the north. And these forty-eight cyclones are what hold the world up. They also sent all kinds of winds up to the Sky to hold up the sky and stars. The Indians have a wind prayer, Eyah-nos-zhini, which is to help these winds hold up the world. Begochiddy told them now to chew up the roots and herbs and then blow this medicine in different directions.

Then Begochiddy took the Ethkaynah-ashi and motioned toward all creation, and it came to life. And the Sun started to rise in the east, and the Sun Spirit's heart started to beat. The Sun and the Moon moved quickly, and the Mountains and Stars slowly, and the eyes of the people in Council were paralyzed at seeing this movement. And everyone was petrified and called out: "What is the matter with our eyes, they won't move!"

Etsay-hashkeh, the Coyote, and Hashjeshjin knew why this happened, and Etsay-hashkeh jumped up and said: "I will explain it to you. The son-in-law and mother-in-law must not look at each other. It is like the stars; the constellation Etsatso is the mother-in-law, and the constellation Dilgeheh is the son-in-law, and these stars must not meet. For the same reason mother-in-law and son-in-law must not see each other, and if they do, their eyes will become blind." When they had understood this, their eyes ceased to be paralyzed.

They named the Earth Spirit, Nahastsan-be-esteen, and the Sun, Johonah-eh, and the Sky Spirit, Yaah-dith-klithy-be-esteen, and the Moon, Klayonah-eh, and the two mountains, Siss-nah-jini and Tsoll-tsilth.

And while they were being named, the Coyote said: "Tsoll-tsilth is my name, and I want it."

But they said: "No, you cannot have it. Your name is Mah-ih (thief)."

He said: "I am not a thief," and he was very angry and sent his spirit to trouble Tsoll-tsilth (Mount Taylor) which began to slide down, so that the gods had to put a lot of small peaks of Malpais (badlands) around the mountain to stop it from slipping, and the little peaks succeeded in holding it, and they are still doing so.

They asked Tsoll-tsilth if he was all right now, and the Mountain said that he was quite comfortable. He cut the hair off from one side of his head so that there are trees on one side only today. Then the Council named all the mountains in their order and they all went where they are today.

First Death and First Movement of Creation

Everything was in its place, but the Earth, Sky, Sun, and Moon did not move, and the Coyote said the reason was that a person was going to die. (Begochiddy told this to the Coyote and the Coyote told the people.) Then the first person died, who was called Etsaydassalini, and at once the Earth and the Sun and Moon began to move again, and the Sun said: "I am glad when a person dies as that is what keeps me moving, and I am glad to keep moving."

Begochiddy planted everything that grew, and made everything that breathed, and took the Ethkay-nah-ashi, and motioned toward all creatures and plants, and they came to life. He appointed the seasons for everything that grew, and they answered: "We will do as we are told." And all creation started and the ants began building houses. The first time that the Sun crossed the sky, it was too near the Earth and it was too hot. The second time it still was too hot. The third time it was still too hot, but the fourth time it was exactly in the right place and it has stayed there ever since.

Etsay-Hasteen asked: "Where has the life gone from the man who died?"

No one knew, so he kept on asking all the people until he came to Begochiddy, who answered him: "I will hunt for it."

So he hunted for a long time but could not find the life that had gone until he looked down into the Third World, and there he saw the man who had died brushing his hair, his face painted red. And Begochiddy came to the people and said: "I have seen the man who died down below in the Third World. I saw him with the shadow of the Ethkay-nah-ashi. You must live holy lives, for the people who do wrong go down to the Burning-Pitch-Place, where there is an enormous monster who devours people." The people who go down there are called Chindi or Devils.

Begochiddy then said to the people: "I am going to heaven now, but I will come back in two days. Watch me go up."

And they all watched him as he went straight up into the air.

At this time Has-estrageh-hasleen died, and he was the second man to die. When Begochiddy came back in two days, he said it was a very beautiful place up there in heaven and that he had seen Has-estrageh-hasleen in a very beautiful place, sitting surrounded by flowers and smelling of them, and Begochiddy said: "All who believe in my word will go up to heaven, but all who do wrong or think wrong will go down to where the pitch is burning."

While Begochiddy was in heaven, he made a man called Begothkai, whom he called his son, and brought back with him to earth. He was a short man, white in flesh, with black eyes and black hair and with a white face.

Begothkai spoke to the people and told them to move to Nahtee-tseel (north of Durango, Colorado) where there are four mountains in a line, and after they had done as he told them then they could live wherever they liked. Then Begochiddy and his son went back to heaven, and Day and Night came to the earth as they come today. Begothkai never has come down again from heaven.

When the people first emerged from the lower world, they had seen a Yeh over on Mount Taylor, Tsoll-tsilth, but he was small and they were not afraid. Now they saw him again, and he had grown very large and had a very big nose, small eyes, and black whiskers on his chin. They realized that he had turned into a giant. When they first saw him, they thought he was a Yeh, but now they knew he was a Yetso or Big Giant. (The reason that the giant lived on Tsoll-tsilth was because Tsoll-tsilth was a badly behaved mountain which had argued about its name and had asked to dress in white shell beads.) The Sun claimed the giant and called him his son, although he really was not related to him, and the Sun took the giant to his home and dressed him with stone shoes and clothing of Bezh, or obsidian, to protect him from his enemies. And he gave him the Lightning Arrow (Iknee-kah) as a weapon for his right hand, and a stone knife for his left hand. When he had dressed him, the Sun took the Yehtso on a streak of lightning and went to Tsoll-tsilth. The giant had a hot spring, Toh-sit-toh, from which he drank, and though the people lived far from this place, when the giant would call "singo," the people were forced to come to him, and then he would eat them. Then the people saw another kind of monster called Dah-il-kadeh who lived at Black Lake (near Pueblo Bonito, New Mexico). This monster had twelve antelopes guarding him, and when the antelope saw any person within reach, they told Dah-il-kadeh, and he ran out and grabbed them and then ran backward on his own track to his den. Dah-il-kadeh looks like a gopher but is enormous. He hunted in all four directions, and the people were very much afraid of him as he was very fierce. They never went near him, but he could often catch them as he could run very fast.

There was an enormous bird, Tseh-nah-hahleh, who lived at Ship Rock, Tseh-ed-ah, who had a very long beak, very large eyes, and his claws were very long and sharp, and he ate people. He had two little ones in his nest whom he had to feed.

There also was a man made of stone who lay stretched out on a hill beside the river just west of the Aztec Ruins. When anyone walked past, he would kick them into the San Juan River, and when they were drowned, he would feed them to his two children. He was called Tseh-ed-ah-eh-delklithy, which means Kicking Rock. His children lived in the river and ate the drowned people.

Also on the top of the Jemez Mountains there was a great hollow place called Nehochee-otso, and there lived a great striped rock which could roll very quickly in any direction and killed people by rolling on them. It was called Tseh-nagi, Rolling Rock.

Then on the east side of Blue Water, New Mexico, there was a red mountain where a lot of black insects lived who killed people by looking at them. They stared at a person until he was paralyzed, and then they ate him. They were called Benan-yah-runi, or Staring-Eyes-That-Kill.

Where the La Plata River meets the San Juan River lived an immense centipede who was very fierce and treacherous, and could run very fast. He had many young ones who helped to eat the people. He was called Sil-dil-hushy-tso, the One-Who-Bites.

There was also a Crushing Rock, or Rocks-That-Come-Together, just west of Taos Mountain. This was called Tseh-ah-kin-dithly.

Dohgah-tyelth, west of the Chama River, was the place of Luka-ih-digishi, the cutting Reeds. Here many trails led into the reeds, and when anyone passed through them, the reeds moved and cut the person into little pieces and ate him. If no one was among the reeds, they remained perfectly quiet.

Another monster was called Tseh-ko, a narrow black canyon north of Taos. If a person tried to step across it, it widened and they fell in and were killed.

Up in the Canjilon Mountains, there was a place called Siss-pai. There were big cactuses called Hoosh-esh-entsiah-etso, and many trails led among them. When people walked through the trails the cactus would close and catch them. They had heads like human beings, and when a person was caught on the spines of the cactus, he stayed there until he dried up.

On the Mancos River lived the Tushgizhi-ent-dil-kizhi, rock Swallows. They were very bad birds. They would rush out at people, striking them and clawing them at once.

At Tsilth-entsah, there lived four bears, Shush-nah-kahi (Bears-

That-Trail). These monsters were killing many people, who were in despair and did not know how to fight them.

The Saving of Created Beings

At Tsilth-nah-ot-zilthy, the small Huerfano Mountain, were living Etsay-Hasteen, Estsa-assun, and Etsay-hashkeh (First Man, First Woman, and Coyote). They were not in danger from the monsters because they went about in a cloud. By this time, the people were being killed off so fast that only a few were left.

And Begochiddy came down from heaven, and when he saw how the people were suffering, he took pity on them and said he would preserve them. He told them he would put a pair of every living creature into a large flute made of big bamboo which belonged to Etsay-Hasteen.

And all the creatures said: "Very well, we are willing to go."

And they got into the flute, and it flew off with them. They flew to Siss-nah-jini, and from there, they flew four times around all the mountains, and then they flew to a big peak called Tsilth-lapai-ah, north of San Francisco Peak. In this peak, there was a large cave. The people got out of the flute and went into the cave and lived there, all except Etsay-hashkeh, Etsay-Hasteen, Estsa-assun and Asheen-assun, who flew away in the flute back to Huerfano Peak. Every day they flew about invisibly, and every night they went back to Huerfano.

They saw a lot of Yehtso-lapai, or grey monsters, walking about. These were large-eyed, fish-eyed, foolish and crazy people, and very bad. They carried baskets on their backs and were very poor and wore grass clothing.

Creation of Estsan-ah-tlehay

Begochiddy asked the four gods in the flute if they were lonely. And they said that they were very lonely now that all the people who had been created were hidden in the cave because of the monsters. So Begochiddy told the First Woman, Estsa-assun: "I will come back in four days and see what can be done." And after four days he came back and said: "This night I will show you."

Then a great Star appeared over Johl-een (Pedernal Mountain). And the star, which was Hashjeshjin (the Fire God), sent a Lightray down to the mountain. Begochiddy came again and asked what they had seen, and they told him that they had seen a bright light on Johl-een. And while they were talking, Hashje-altye (the Talking God) came dressed in a rainbow and a shiny feather headdress. And he spoke four times to them. The people told him to go and see why there was light on the mountain, and he said: "Very well, I will go and find out about it."

When Hashje-altye came to Johl-een, he saw the Lightray connecting the mountain and the sky, and looking like an immense shining cloud or rainbow. Hashje-altye went towards the mountain and heard the Bluebird, Dohleh, singing. And he came to the mountain from the west side, and he heard all sorts of birds singing. And when he came from the north, he heard the pollen or corn bird, Ahn-enteni. Then he went back from the north, to the west, then to the south, then to the east side, and stood there. And then he went up to the mountain, and there he found a very fine, newly born baby girl, with flowers surrounding her. Hashje-altye was very glad to see this and went back to tell Begochiddy and the others what he had found. Begochiddy knew all about the baby, as he had seen it, and he said to the people: "It is the child of the Earth Spirit and the Sky Spirit."

Then the gods went and found the baby, bringing gifts with them. Estsa-assun brought a white shell basket, Etsay-Hasteen a fine water bowl; Asheen-assun (Salt Woman) brought soap root. They were going to wash the baby then, but before doing so, they asked all the mountains and peaks if they could take care of it and wash it, but the mountains and peaks could not agree as to which should undertake the care of the child, and so all refused. Begochiddy came down and told the gods to take the baby to Lukasahkah-tso (Alamo), and wash the baby there at that spring, and then to take her back to Tsilth-nah-ot-zilthy (Huerfano Peak), and there to make a hogahn out of mirage to be called Hadahonigay-be-hogahn.

They did all that Begochiddy commanded, and loved the baby very much, and guarded it closely. And the mountains also loved the baby.

They made a cradle of the straight lightning for it and placed a rainbow at the foot of the cradle, and they decorated the cradle with a rainbow, and the bow over the top of the cradle was made of a rainbow. The Salt Woman was sent to get something soft for the baby to lie on, and she shredded bark for it, and this same bark is used today for babies' cradles. The cradle was called Away-estsa.

The robe in which the baby was wrapped was made of a beautifully patterned cloud, and over it, they wrapped the baby in another white cloud robe, and used a very fine white rock powder to rub in all the baby's creases. The Salt Woman called the baby her sister. They then motioned to the baby with the Ethkaynah-ashi and gave it life, and the baby started to cry.

Hashje-altye spoke to the others and said: "How can we feed the baby?" And they tried to feed it on pollen, but it did not agree with the baby, so Hashje-altye said: "It would be better to give the baby to Hashje-ba-ahd (the female Yeh), and she would know how to bring it up and take care of it." The gods who had the baby would not agree to this. They loved the baby so much they would not give it up to anyone, and they said they could feed the baby on the pollen of the white shell. So Hashje-altye agreed that they should take care of it. Hashje-hogahn (the House God) also asked for the baby, as he had daughters who would take care of it and feed it from the pollen of the afterglow of the sunset, but the gods refused to let him have the child. They fed the baby with the white inside bark of the cedar tree mixed with pollen, but the baby did not like it and spat it out. Then they fed her with the white shell pollen and the flower pollen, and she liked this and flourished.

When she was two years old, she was able to walk about, and one of the Yehtso-lapai, a Grey Monster, tried to steal her, but fortunately Etsay-Hasteen saw the Yehtso climbing up the mountain looking for the baby. The Yehtso could not see the baby, but he found her tracks, and Etsay-Hasteen said to the monster: "There is no baby here. I made these tracks that you have found with my hands." Four times Etsay-Hasteen drove the Yehtso-lapai away.

Asheen-assun, the Salt Woman, was the nurse of the baby and guarded her. And once upon a time, a good many of the Yehtso-lapai managed to see the Salt Woman with the baby, and they tried to climb up the mountain to reach them but found it too difficult. After this happened, Etsay-Hasteen planted a great many little cactus plants around the mountain, so that when the Yehtso-lapai attempted to climb over them, they cried out with pain and did not dare to cross the cactus in order to steal the baby.

When she was about six years old and had lost her baby teeth, they made her another set of teeth of white shell and told her when she rose in the morning to throw her old teeth toward the east.

Maiden Ceremony for Estsan-ah-tlehay

When she was sixteen years old, they had the Maiden Ceremony for her called Hozhonigi, or Making-the-Path-of-Life-Beautiful. They dressed her in white shell shoes, fine deer-skin robes, and the finest sort of shell and turquoise ornaments. Her hair was parted in the middle and hung down tied at the back halfway to the ends. They invited Kay-des-tizhi, the Man-Wrapped-in-a-Rainbow, and he came and brought many different shell dishes and food, and also he brought her a baby lamb; and all the gods came; also the Yeh.

The ceremony began with a race between the Salt Woman and the girl before sunrise every morning for four days. On the night of the fourth day, they sang the Creation Song, which has twenty-four verses. Etsay-Hasteen sang it first and the others after him, and they sang until daybreak. Etsay-Hasteen also had a song he sang while the girl and woman raced before sunrise, which is called Sheyash-estsa-sohni, or Young-Woman's-Race. They told the Earth Spirit about this ceremony, and he sent the white and red paint with which they painted her cheeks red, and they painted two small white stripes on each cheek. They sang of painting the maiden, Zhan-sheya-yanez-nuchee. Begochiddy told the people that he wanted them to paint their faces in the same way. Those who begin the painting of their faces at the top and paint down to the chin signify that they are asking for rain; those who paint from the chin up to the forehead are asking for anything that grows. So they painted their faces, and brought many robes, and piled them in a heap on top of one another at the door of the Mirage Hogahn where the girl lived.

Then she lay face down flat on this pile of robes, and her hair covered her whole body. Estsa-assun stroked her hair and face and body to make her fine and strong. After that, they gave her the lamb which Kay-des-tizhi had brought her, and she held it to her breast as she lay on the pile of blankets.

Begochiddy asked the people what name they were going to give this girl, but they all stood silent. And while they watched her, she grew older and older until she was a bent old woman, and even as they watched her, she grew a little younger again, and before their eyes she changed four times from youth to age, but at the fourth change she remained about twenty years old, and she was very beautiful. Begochiddy named her White Shell Woman, Yolthkai-estsan, and the rest of the people called her by that name. From this time onward, she would always be able to grow old or young as she desired, and so she was called also Estsan-ah-tlehay, or Changing Woman.

Then she rose from the pile of robes and gave the lamb back to Kay-des-tizhi, the Man-Wrapped-in-a-Rainbow. And the people turned their backs to her, and she went to each one in turn, and took their heads in her hands, and lifted them a little to thank them for their gifts. Begochiddy gave her a big basket full of flowers, and she gave the flowers to the people who put them in their hair, and all went away again very happy and thankful. In the basket of flowers which she had passed around, there were a lot of poison weeds named Johnjilway, Toh-o-whetso, Asgai-binee, Ajah-tohee, but no one received them; they only received the good flowers and the poison weeds were taken back into the hogahn.

Mating of the Sun and Estsan-ah-tlehay

One day the maiden was gathering wood and suddenly felt someone touch the bundle of wood which she carried. She was terrified, dropped her wood, and ran home.

When she got there, Estsa-assun asked her what was the matter, and reassured her, and told her to go back again and get some more wood. She was twenty-two years old now, and though at first she did not know who had touched her, she found out that it was the Sun Spirit who had fallen in love with her.

After this, during six months, she and the Sun Spirit did not see each other and were separated; and this separation was called Toh-n'del-kous.

Birth of Nayenezgani and Tohbachischin

About six months after the separation of the maiden and the Sun, twins were born to her called Nayenezgani, who was the elder, and Tohbachischin, and they had the same sort of cradle as was made for their mother. They did not eat anything for four days after they were born. They gave them cedar bark at first to eat, but it did not agree with them, and after four days, their mother began to feed them, and they flourished. At two years old, they could walk and play around the hogahn. It is said that at Huerfano Peak (Tsilth-nah-ot-zilthy), where they lived, the tracks of the boys are still to be seen. Hashje-altye and Begochiddy came often to see the boys, as they loved them very much, and at four years old, they were both quite big and strong. When they were seven years old, they both lost their teeth, and their mother put white shell teeth in the place of the ones they had lost. They threw away their old teeth towards the east, and it is said that all teeth that are thus thrown away are given to the Badger, Tabasteen.

When they were sixteen years old, they were quite grown-up, and they looked so much alike no one could tell them apart. They wanted very much to find out who their father was. They asked this four times before the Sun had risen, but their mother was ashamed to tell them. But when the Sun had come up about half-way, she pointed to it and said: "That is your father."

Etsay-Hasteen made the twins bows and arrows, and they went about hunting and enjoying themselves. Once in their wanderings they came close to the edge of the mountain, and they saw a Yehtso, a Grey Monster, coming up, and they shot at him with their bows and arrows, and he was so frightened that he ran away.

One day when they were out hunting, Begochiddy met them and, sitting down between them, said: "The Sun is your father, and you must go and visit him." To help them, and to tell them what would happen in the future, and to show them the way, he gave them wind spirits, Niltche-beyazh. And he gave Nayenezgani, the elder, the rainbow, Natseẹlit, to carry him wherever he wanted to go. And he gave Tohbachischin a ray of light, Shah-bekloth. He told the boys that, when they came to their father's house, they would be shown all sorts of clothing and other things, but that they must choose only the flint armor, Bezh; the lightning-arrows, Iknee-kah;

and the stone knife; also the big cyclones and the big hail; and the kehtahn or magic cigarette named Kehtahn-de-konth; and he repeated: "You must be sure to ask for that." (Their mother, Estsan-ah-tlehay, did not know that they were starting on this journey.)

Beginning of the Journey to the Sun

Then Nayenezgani stood on the rainbow, and Tohbachischin stood on the ray of light, and Begochiddy breathed on the rainbow and the ray of light and started them on their way. After flying some distance through the air, they walked on the earth again for some distance, but they came to a great sand dune called Sals-ah which they could not cross on foot. So they mounted their rainbow and ray of light and were carried over that obstacle. They walked again for some distance but had to mount into the air on their magic rainbow and ray to cross a very big canyon. Then they walked again until they came to a very big cactus, when again they used their magic arrows. And again they walked until they were stopped by many reeds, and they crossed them in the same magic way.

Again they walked on and came to a big river. At the edge of the river, they found a lot of water bugs who asked the twins where they were going, and the boys said that they were going to cross the river, and the bugs said: "We will help you." And they bunched themselves together, and took the boys on their backs, and carried them over.

After they had crossed the river, they met a meadowlark who asked them: "Where are you going, my grandsons? Your father is very angry, so I will give you a song to help you when you meet him." So the meadowlark sang a song to them, and they went on their way.

Suddenly a woman who had a spiderweb in her hand jumped out of the ground before them, and she was the Spider Woman. She invited the boys to come into her home, but the boys thought the doorway was too small and that they could not get in. The Spider Woman knew what they were thinking, so she blew four times at the doorway, and each time that she blew, the doorway grew larger until finally it was large enough for the boys to enter. The Spider Woman said to them: "Your father is not kind, so I will teach you a song to help you, and also give you an eagle's pinfeather which will protect you."

The boys went on their way until they met four old women who asked them: "Where are you coming from?" The boys pointed to their home, and the old woman said to the boys: "Your father is not kind, so we will give you a song to help you." These were the first old people in the world, and if they had not met the boys, no one would ever grow old now. The twins went on and met an older woman who would not speak to them, and later, they met a still older woman. Then the twins came to the Daybreak, and they went on under it until they came to the After-Glow-of-Sunset and went on under it, then under the Dusk, then under the Darkness, until they came to a place where many children were playing, and this place was called Yeh-kai-beyazhi, and they crossed this place on their rainbow and light ray. And they then went up into the Black Sky and came to the Turquoise House, Hogahn-doklizh, which is always in darkness.

On the wall outside near the door of the house was a large hook on which the Sun was hung, while the Spirit of the Sun lived inside the house. In the Turquoise House were four rooms, one east, one south, one west, and one north, and there were many little Suns there, and all sorts of bright lights to make it light. Two Thunderbirds, Iknee, were guarding the door, but the boys entered the house without being molested by the guards although they saw the twins. The second guard over the house was the Water Monster, Teoltsodi, and the third guard was the big snake, Kleeshtso. The fourth guard was the mountain lion, Nashtui-l'tso, and the boys passed all of them.

Test of the Twins by the Sun

Inside on the east side of the house there was a black cloud rolled up, on the south side a blue cloud, on the west a yellow cloud, and on the north a white cloud. The twins met the Moon Spirit there, though the Moon itself was not present as it was wandering about. And the Spirit asked them: "What are you doing here, my boys? Your father is a fierce man, and I will try to protect you." So the Spirit wrapped the two boys in the white cloud to hide them.

After they were hidden in the white cloud, the Sun Spirit came in and asked the Moon Spirit: "Who was speaking?"

And the Moon Spirit answered: "No one except myself."

The Sun Spirit did not believe this, and went to the black cloud, and unrolled it, but found nothing there, and he unrolled the south cloud and the west cloud, and finally in the north cloud, he found the boys. He seized them by the hair of their heads and threw them against some great spikes of obsidian which were turned edge-wise like knives set in the floor at the east side of the hogahn. He said: "I hope these boys are my sons" (for if they were really his sons they would not be hurt by anything). They were not harmed by the knives, and then the Sun Spirit threw them onto the knives on the south, west, and north, and they were still unharmed.

The Sun Spirit called the Moon Spirit and said: "Uncle, heat the sweat house."

So the Moon Spirit heated the sweat house, and on one side, he dug a hole large enough to contain the two boys and covered it with a little Moon. He brought the boys over to the sweat house and showed them the hole where they could hide, and they hid themselves in it. Then the Sun Spirit came to the house bringing a jug of water and poured it on a bar of obsidian which had been heated red hot, and it filled the house with much steam, and he asked the boys: "Are you too warm in there?"

And the boys answered: "No."

He asked this of the boys four times, and they answered each time: "No, we are all right," so the Sun Spirit went back to his hogahn, and the boys came out of the sweat house.

Each night while they were at the Sun's house, they slept on the roof, and they had a robe of white clouds to cover them, and the Sun Spirit gave them another robe also, but they were very cold there and would have frozen except that the Otter Woman came and gave them her fur robe to spread over them. It hailed and stormed all night, and the Sun thought that they would be frozen, but thanks to the fur robe which the Otter Woman gave them they were warm.

When the Sun went into his home again, he filled a turquoise pipe, a white shell pipe, an abalone pipe, and a jet pipe with poison smoke. On their way back to the Sun's house from the sweat house, the twins met a caterpillar who gave them some medicine weeds to eat so that they could not be killed if they smoked the poison pipes of the Sun. Back in the Sun's house again, the boys were given a blue pipe to smoke, and the Sun lighted it with a little Sun. They smoked all of the pipes easily.

Finding that he could not kill them with the poison smoke, the Sun Spirit caught the boys by the hair and threw them into a big black jar on the east side of the room. He then hung a huge stone by a stream of water to the roof over the jar and let the stone fall to crush the twins, but when he looked into the jar, he saw the boys in it unharmed. He tried this four times, and even made the great stone drop more heavily, but he could not hurt the twins. Then he took the boys into his arms, holding one on either side of him, for he knew now that they were really his sons, because they had not been harmed by his tests.

The Sun Spirit had four children by a spirit woman named Yoodi-yenai, who had been in the Fourth World. Her eldest daughter was called Turquoise Girl, Doklizhe-etahdeh, and the younger was called White Shell Girl, Yolthkai-etahdeh. The older boy was called Abalone Boy, Dichithli-eshki, and the younger boy was called Jet Boy, Baszhini-eshki. The Sun Spirit said to his daughters: "Bring some water to your brothers," and the Turquoise Girl brought a blue basket and a jug of water, and the White Shell Girl brought a white basket and a jug of water, and also they brought soap root, and the twins washed their hair, and their sisters bathed them and dried them first with fine white cornmeal and then with corn pollen. Then the Sun and his spirit wife went to the eastern room and brought sweet-smelling flowers with which they rubbed the twins. And they were made beautiful and looked just like the other children of the Sun. And they sat down on a turquoise bench. The Sun Spirit told his daughters to feed the twins, and they gave them Yolthkai-tahn (cornmeal mush, ceremonially called White-Shell-Food).

The Sun Spirit then asked the twins: "Why did you come to me?"

And they answered: "There are monsters killing all of our people, and we want to be able to kill them."

The Sun Spirit did not answer but took the boys to the east room which was reached by steps. He opened the door, and there they saw many rainbows, and the Sun Spirit asked the twins if that was what they wanted, but the boys said: "No, we do not want that sort of thing."

Then the Sun took them to a door at the south and opened it, and there were many plants, corn, beans, and so forth. And the Sun Spirit said: "Is that what you wanted?"

The boys said: "No."

So the west door was opened, and there they saw clothing and jewelry, and the Sun asked them: "Did you come for this sort of thing?"

And they said: "No," but the boys had forgotten what they wanted, and the Sun then showed them many more things.

Then Niltche-beyazh, the Spirit Wind, spoke in their ears and said: "Begochiddy told you to ask for flint armor and the other weapons."

So they said to the Sun: "We want the flint armor and the stone knife, lightning arrows, cyclones, hail, and the magic kehtahn."

The Sun said to them: "What do you want them for? They are dangerous."

And they answered: "We want to dress in that armor and use the weapons to kill the giants and the monsters."

When the twins answered thus, the Sun Spirit sat down with his head in his hands and said sadly: "You must not kill your brother," for he claimed the giants as his children. But finally he decided to grant their request and said: "Very well, I will give what you have asked for." And he taught them how to wear the armor, and how to shoot the lightning arrows, and how to use the stone knife, the big hail, the cyclones, and also how to use the magic kehtahn. And they then told him how they were going to kill the monsters, the bears, and other creatures who were harming the people.

Then the Sun Spirit gave them the gifts that they had asked for, and they started to go back to Tsoll-tsilth on the clouds, the Sun accompanying them. And when they reached there, they rested above the mountain sitting on the clouds, and the Sun Spirit asked them many questions to test their cleverness. He pointed to Siss-nah-jini and asked them its name and the boys answered correctly. The Sun asked the names of all the mountains, and they named them correctly. He also pointed to Huerfano Peak below, and the boys recognized their home, so the Sun was satisfied that they were intelligent and asked them no more questions.

Killing of the Giant

They were preparing to go to kill the monsters, but the Sun Spirit said to them: "Let me try first to kill the giant." The twins descended on the lightning to the earth at Bahkse-hotetsa, which is near Tsoll-tsilth (Mount Taylor), and then went up to the top of the mountain, carried by the lightning and the rainbow. They sat down on a rock called Azeth which is just south of Mount Taylor (near Grants, New Mexico), and the Wind Spirit told them to hurry and put on their stone armor. So they put it on, and when they had done so, suddenly to the east they saw the giant's forehead appearing, then he passed out of sight again. Then he appeared at the south, then at the west, then at the north, and each time they saw him more plainly until, when he appeared at the north, they could see the whole of him except his feet, and then he disappeared in a flash and went back to his spring, Toh-sit-toh, where he stopped to drink, his hands on the ground.

The boys mounted the magic lightning and rainbow and flew over the giant as he drank, and he saw their reflections in the spring and rose up. They approached from the east and the giant said: "What fine boys, I must have them."

They answered together: "What a big giant, we must have him."

This enraged the giant, and he seized his stone knife and threw it at the boys. It passed under them because the Wind Spirit had warned them, and they rose on the rainbow as the giant threw the knife. When the knife hit the ground, the boys seized it and went around to the south of the giant, and as they came towards him from that direction, the Wind Spirit warned them to bend down, while another stone knife, thrown by the giant, flew over their heads. They picked up this knife also and went to attack him from the west. The giant threw another knife at them, but warned by the Wind Spirit, they escaped it by rising into the air, and they picked up that knife. Then they were attacked from the north, and escaped again, and picked up that knife also.

Now the Sun sent help in the form of a big black cloud which dropped down on the giant bringing a black cyclone. And lightning came from the cloud and broke the giant's suit of stone armor on all four sides, and Hashjeshjin (the Fire God), who was still in the Third World, sent up a volcano with fire coming out of it to help the twins. And the giant shook all over.

Then the twins took their lightning arrows and shot them through the giant, and the arrows threw the giant's heart to a place northeast of Bluewater, and it is still to be seen there in the form of a big black volcanic rock.

From the place where his heart and body fell, the blood started running in rivers in different directions, so the twins drew a line with their stone knife through the blood and made a deep valley to divide the blood streams, for if they should join, the giant would live again; and where the blood settled is now a plain of volcanic rock.

The boys scalped the giant and took the sinew from the back of his neck, and they cut off the point of his heart. Tsoll-tsilth claimed the body, and it is still in the mountain. Begochiddy appeared then and said: "You have done well," and then he blew on the giant and turned his body and blood to rock.

The twins went back to their home at Tsilth-nah-ot-zilthy (Huerfano Peak), and greeted their mother and the other three women who were there, and all the women danced with joy when they saw the boys come. The name of the dance is Chono-teen. Etsay-Hasteen played the big flute, and then he made the wand such as is now used in the N'dah (or Squaw Dance) ceremony. And they carved a wand with a bow symbol on one side and a scalp symbol on the other side of it. This wand is called Ahralth-tseen now, but it used to be called Ahtsee-des-tseen.

The twins said: "We have killed the giant, Mother."

And she answered them: "Oh, no, you could not have killed such an enormous giant. He has stone clothing and so many knives that you could not hurt him." (Their mother really knew that they had killed the giant, but pretended that she did not.)

Next morning they had their breakfast, and then they placed in the middle of the hogahn the white cloud with the male rain (heavy rain), also the cyclone, also the hail, and the burning kehtahn. And Nayenezgani, the older twin, said to the younger: "I am going to kill the monsters, meanwhile you must watch this burning kehtahn, and when I am in great danger, it will burn very bright and fast; then you must come and help me at once."

Then Nayenezgani asked: "Where shall I find Dah-il-kadeh?" (the great monster that looks like a gopher). And he was told that it lived at Black Lake, so he set off to kill it, and when he walked, the ground trembled under his feet he was so powerful, and he carried the fire stick, Nestrahnihi.

Killing of Dah-il-kadeh

The monster was watching in all directions and also was guarded by twelve antelopes, but they could not see Nayenezgani because he was flying on the rainbow, and he landed near the monster and walked around to discover some place from which he could attack it. As he went along, he met the Gopher, who ran back into his hole, then came out again, and kept on running in and out again four times, but finally said to the boy: "What is the matter, my grandson?"

And Nayenezgani answered: "I want to kill this monster, Dah-il-kadeh, but I cannot reach him."

And the Gopher said to him, "I am willing to go near him—I am not afraid of him."

And the boy said: "If you will help me to reach him, you may have his skin."

The Gopher made a hole and burrowed under the ground to the monster, then he made another hole deeper in the earth, another deeper still, and the fourth tunnel was a very deep one and was dug under the monster's heart. When the Gopher reached the monster, he ate off the hair under his heart, and the monster felt this and moved, saying: "What is under me?"

And the Gopher answered: "I am getting fur to wrap my children who are cold."

Then the Gopher went back to Nayenezgani and told him that he was ready. And they both went into the tunnel, and when they reached the monster's heart, and saw it, and heard it beating, the boy took a lightning arrow and shot it through the heart. The monster jumped up and destroyed the lower tunnel with his horns, but as he did so, the boy ran to the next tunnel, and when the monster destroyed that, the boy escaped to the third tunnel, and when this was destroyed, he hid in the upper tunnel and the monster tore up half of the tunnel in which the boy was hidden, but fell over dead before he could reach the boy.

The antelope guards were rushing around the monster looking for Nayenezgani, and when they saw him, he lit some cedar bark with his fire stick and threw a piece to the east and all the antelopes ran after it, then he threw another burning piece of bark to the south, and they ran after that, and another to the west, and another piece to the north. When they had chased after that, they were so tired that they were helpless, and the boy took his stone knife and killed all but two of them, and he told these two antelopes that they must behave better in the future. He told them this four times, and they agreed that they would be good.

Nayenezgani was still afraid to go near the monster, and the Gopher said: "I will find out if he is dead. I will run around on his horns." So he ran from one horn to the other and proved that the monster was dead. And Nayenezgani went up to him and scalped him, and took the sinews of the legs and neck and took his stomach and filled it with blood. Also he cut off his horns which were the shape of the antelope horns. Though he was very large, the monster had a very small eye. Nayenezgani told the Gopher that he could help himself to the rest of the monster, and the Gopher brushed himself with the blood, making himself look so much like the monster that, when you look at the Gopher now, you can tell how the Dah-il-kadeh looked.

Nayenezgani went home, and as he came near, he gave the god-call, Yo-ho-ho-ho and also Ya-ha-ha-ha, and his mother and the other women met him with dancing. Etsay-Hasteen played his flute, and they sang. They hung the scalp of the Dah-il-kadeh on the cedar wand, Aralth-tseen, and as they did so, the wand threw off sparks. Then Nayenezgani told his mother about his adventures, and she pretended as before that he could not have killed the monster, but he convinced her that it was true, and he spent the night there.

Killing of the Great Bird

Next day he clothed himself in stone armor and asked his mother and grandmother where he could find the Great Bird, Tseh-nah-hahleh. And his mother told him that it was very dangerous to hunt the bird. Nayenezgani, however, started on his way, taking with him the skin of the Dah-il-kadeh and the blood enclosed in the monster's stomach, and the earth shook as he went. The rainbow carried him towards the home of the Great Bird on top of Ship Rock. Before he reached it, he dressed himself in the skin of the Dah-il-kadeh, and he carried the monster's stomach full of blood inside his clothing. The Great Bird saw him coming and flew towards him making much noise, flying over him four times. Then she caught up Nayenezgani in her claws, and carried him to Ship Rock, circling it four times, and then threw him down between the two peaks. Nayenezgani would have been killed by the fall except for the fact that the feather which the Spider Woman had given him enabled him to fall slowly.

When he lit on the rock, he tore open the stomach full of blood, and the Great Bird thought she had killed him and so flew off the nest, telling her little ones to eat Nayenezgani, as he was dead. Nayenezgani lay still, and the little birds came nearer to him, but he said: "Sh-sh," and frightened them away.

They called out to their mother: "Shemah (Mother), this human being is not dead, for he said 'Sh-sh' to us."

But the Great Bird said: "That is nonsense. Go on and eat. The noise you heard was the sound of his fall."

So the Great Bird flew away to the west over the mountains, and when she had gone, Nayenezgani got up, and went to their nest, and called the little birds to him, and they were frightened, and went back to their nest, and began to cry. Nayenezgani told them to be quiet and that, if they made a noise, he would kill them.

The oldest bird came to him, and Nayenezgani took hold of him, and pushed his beak down, and made his wings a different shape, and painted his wings and tail white, and told him to go south and live there and be good, and not do any harm to anyone anymore, and he became the first eagle. Nayenezgani called the smaller bird to him four times before he would come, and then Nayenezgani gave him a long pair of ears and told him that he was to be the owl and that, if he harmed the earth people, he would kill him. And he sent him north to the La Plata Mountains to a place which was to be his home, called Saltahn-iskai, near Pagosa Peak. And the owl was very tired when he reached his new home.

Nayenezgani looked about to find a place in which to hide so that he could kill the parent birds, but the only place he could find was in the nest, and so he hid there. Then the male rain started, and he saw the father bird flying back with something in his claws, and when he came nearer, Nayenezgani saw that he was carrying a handsome young man who was dressed in fine jewelry and many bracelets. And the bird dropped the man, and when he fell, the turquoise jewelry flew in every direction. The father bird then lit on the peak, but before he folded his wings, Nayenezgani shot him and saw that the young man whom the bird had dropped on the peak was a Taos Indian. From the west began a light female rain, and the mother bird flew in, carrying a young and pretty girl dressed in white shell beads. And she dropped the girl on the rock. Just as the mother bird lit on the peak, Nayenezgani shot her with a lightning arrow, and the bird fell dead from the peak.

Nayenezgani now looked about to find a way down from the peak, and below he saw a bat whose name was Jahbunny-estsan (Bat Woman), and he said to her: "Grandmother, help me down, and I will give you a feather." She hid four times and would not answer. Finally she told him to go to the other side of the peak, and then she appeared to Nayenezgani with a basket on her back, upheld by spider webs. She danced about when she reached the top of the peak and said to him: "Now get into my basket."

But Nayenezgani answered: "The strings are too small, they will break under my weight."

But she said: "No, I can carry a very heavy load with these webs."

Nayenezgani was afraid and would not get into the basket, so the Bat Woman told him to fill it with big rocks, and he did so, and the strings of the spider web still held, although they buzzed with the strain. Nayenezgani was convinced that the Bat Woman could carry him, and he took the stones out of the basket, and went over to the edge of the peak, and got into the basket. The Bat Woman told him to shut his eyes, and she began to go down. Halfway down, the Bat Woman stopped on a small ledge and walked back and forth while Nayenezgani wondered whether they were on the ground or not, but he could not see as she had told him to keep his eyes shut.

He grew so nervous that he opened his eyes, and at once, they both fell to the ground, but fortunately the shelf on which they had been was not far up the cliff. The Bat Woman was so angry that she struck Nayenezgani with a cane she held in her hand, because he had opened his eyes. Then he got out of the basket and went to where the Great Bird had fallen. He pulled out twelve of his tail feathers, doing the same to the female bird, and he scalped both birds with his stone knife, and told the Bat Woman to help herself to the feathers that remained, and she filled her basket with small feathers.

Nayenezgani warned her not to go through the sunflower place as she would regret it, and he set off towards home, but as he went, he watched the Bat Woman because he saw she was going straight to the sunflower place. When she reached there, all the feathers in the basket blew out, and she lost them all. She went back to find the dead birds again, thinking that she would find more feathers, but Nayenezgani did not wait to see if she got any. He mounted his rainbow and went home, where his return was celebrated in the same way as it had been before.

Destruction of the Kicking Rock

Next day after breakfast, having found out from his mother where he should go, he started off to Tseh-ed-ah-eh-delkithly (the Rock-That-Kicks-People-Into-the-River). He saw a man lying on his back with his head on a bluff and his feet near the river, and he was pulling the whiskers out of his chin. When Nayenezgani tried to pass, he kicked at him, and Nayenezgani said: "What is the matter, Sechai (Grandfather)?"

The Rock Man said: "My leg was cramped and I had to kick to straighten it out." Four times he was questioned and he answered four times.

After that Nayenezgani took his stone knife, and hit the Rock Man on the head, and cut through his breast, hips and legs, chopping him into four pieces and then scalping him.

The Rock Man's children lived in the river, and Nayenezgani threw the pieces of the Rock Man down to them and heard them quarreling for the pieces of meat, saying: "That is my piece," not knowing that they were eating their own father. Then Nayenezgani went down into the river and killed all the children except two. One was called Kahtsen (Alligator) and Nayenezgani said to him: "You must never hurt anyone again, will you promise this?"

And the alligator answered: "I am not sure."

Nayenezgani asked this four times, but the alligator would not promise.

The other child who was spared was called Siss-'tyel (Turtle), and was told to be good in the future, as he would be used for medicine by men, and his shell would be used to drink out of and also to make medicine in, and the turtle agreed to this and said that he would always be good. So Nayenezgani went home on the rainbow, and they danced and celebrated his return as before.

Destruction of Rolling Rock

The next morning, Nayenezgani asked where he would find Tseh-ehi (the Rolling Rock), and his mother told him that it was in the Jemez Mountains, so he went there and looked at it from a peak nearby. When Nayenezgani tried to approach it, the Rock began to roll towards him, and he shot his lightning arrow at the Rock from the east, but could not hit it, and the Rock then rolled back to its den. Then Nayenezgani shot at it from the south and managed to knock a little splinter from it while the Rock pursued him. He then approached the Rock from the west, and the same thing happened, and also from the north, and at the end, he only managed to knock off a few pieces and could not injure it, and meanwhile it kept chasing him while he was barely able to avoid it.

At his home at Huerfano, the magic kehtahn began to burn very brightly, which showed that Nayenezgani was in great danger. So they sent hail, big rain, and cyclones to attack the Rock. And the water soaked it, and Hashjeshjin burnt it with his fire, and then hit it with a stone knife, and large pieces were broken off it. The Rock tried to escape them, but they chased it into a mountain from which it burst out as though from a volcano, and finally they chased the Rock four times around the earth, while it grew smaller and smaller, until at last it fell into the Grand Canyon, where it now is. After taking its scalp, the three went home—Nayenezgani and Hashjeshjin with Mah-ih-degishi (Spirit of the Scalp).

Destruction of Staring-Eyes-That-Kill

The next hunting by Nayenezgani was of the monsters called Benan-yah-runi (Staring-Eyes-That-Kill), who lived at Tsilth-lachee, Red Mountain.

Asheen-assun, the Salt Woman, brought Nayenezgani a lump of salt and told him how to use it in killing these monsters. And she told him to take his fire sticks also. As he came near where the Staring-Eyes-That-Kill lived, he found a great many of their tracks and followed them to where they lived in a cave, and they all stared at him, never closing their eyes. Nayenezgani made a fire with his fire sticks and threw a handful of salt into the fire, which exploded into the monsters' eyes, blinding them, and they had to shut their eyes to rub the salt and fire out of them. Then Nayenezgani took his stone knife and killed them all, except two which crept into a little crack in the wall of the cave. One of these he made into a Screech Owl, Gloutrah-nasjah, and the other he called Nah-zunni, Snow Bug. He told both of these never to harm people anymore, and they agreed. And he sent the Screech Owl to the prairies, where he was to live in a hollow in the ground. And he sent the Snow Bug to travel on the snow in the winter forever. Then he went home again, and they celebrated in the same way with dancing and song. He told them how he had killed all of the Staring-Eyes-That-Kill. Every time he returned home, he hung the scalps of the monsters he had killed on the scalp stick.

Destruction of the Great Centipedes

After breakfast the next morning, he started out to kill the Sil-dil-hushy-tso (Great Centipedes), and they told him that they lived at a place called Tseh-negleen (Water-Meeting-Place) on the La Plata River near Farmington.

So he went there and found a lot of centipedes who, as they walked, bowed themselves up in the middle and then could spring a great distance to catch their victims. The largest centipede jumped at Nayenezgani but could not bite through the stone armor, and Nayenezgani seized his stone knife, and cut him into little pieces, and then killed all the rest of them and their little ones except a pair, a male and a female, and these he let go, telling them to behave themselves and never harm anyone. He scalped the largest centipede and went home, where he hung the scalp on the scalp stick, and they held the usual celebration.

Destruction of Crushing Rocks

The next morning he went to Chustoh-ba-ahd, south of Taos, where he wanted to destroy the Crushing Rocks, Tseh-ah-kindithly. And he rode on his Rainbow and took with him the horns of the Dah-il-kadeh. When the Rocks tried to crush him, he would evade them on his Rainbow and the Rocks could not crush him. He did this four times, and then he took the horns of the Dah-il-kadeh and put them across between the Rocks which prevented them from coming together. He then threw his fire between the Rocks and heated them so hot that, when he hit them with his stone knife, they splintered into many pieces. Before he left, he motioned toward the splintered rocks and said: "Hereafter, you will be used for the colored sands of which our sand paintings will be made." And this colored rock which Nayenezgani burned is what the Indians now use for their paintings. Then he went home and was received with rejoicing.

Destruction of Cutting Reeds and Other Monsters

The next morning after breakfast, he went to destroy the Cutting Reeds, Luka-degizh, which were at Toh-gay-tyelth, a round peak west of Taos. He took with him his fire sticks, and when he came to the little canyon where the Reeds lived, he pretended to enter on one of the many trails, and the Reeds tried to catch him, waving and clashing together, but four times they missed him. When he tried to cut the Reeds down with his stone knife, he found it was impossible, so he used his fire sticks and burned them all up except two. These he cautioned to be good in the future and he told them that the earth people would use them in their ceremonies. The two Reeds agreed to this, and Nayenezgani took the scalp from the largest Reed, and went home, and told his mother that he had burned all the Cutting Reeds, and then they celebrated.

Then he went to destroy the Canyon-That-Spreads-Apart, Tseh-ko, which is also near Taos. Four times he avoided being dropped into the Canyon as it spread, and then he put four obsidian stones across it and fastened them together to hold the Canyon steady. He told the Canyon that it must be good and not engulf people and that the earth people would use it in their ceremonies. And the Indians pray now to this Canyon. He then went home and they celebrated as before.

The next day he went to destroy the Cactus-That-Catches, Hoosh-entsah-etso, which grew at Siss-pai (near Canjilon). And he destroyed the Cactus with his stone knife and burned all except the little ones which he preserved. And he told them to be good and that they would be used in the ceremonies. Then he went home to his mother.

Next he went to kill the bad Rock Swallows, Tush-gizhi-ent-dilkizhi, who lived near the Mancos River in one of the canyons near Mesa Verde. When Nayenezgani went into this canyon, the birds swooped down on him, and he shot his lightning arrows at them but could not hit them, as they flew too quickly. Then they tried to hurt him, but his stone armor protected him. At home, at Huerfano, the magic kehtahn began to burn brightly, warning Tohbachischin. And he blew four times toward his brother. And the cyclones, hail, thunder, and also the white cloud on which Tohbachischin usually rode all went to help Nayenezgani.

Meanwhile Nayenezgani was running from the birds, who followed him in clouds like a swarm of bees. Then rain came from the white cloud, and the cyclones swept the birds aside, and the hailstones struck them, so all were killed except two little ones. Nayenezgani told these two little birds to be good and do no harm, and the birds promised to do so. So the god let them live in the Canyon peacefully. Then Nayenezgani went home, and they celebrated.

Next Nayenezgani went to find the Bears-That-Trail, Shush-nah-Kahi. There were four of these bears, and they lived on a mountain called Tsilth-entsah, near the Blanco River about four miles east of Farmington. When the god came there and went up the mountain, he met a strange-looking girl named Shikinh-shush-nah-tlehay (Changing-Bear-Maiden), who had red eyes and carried a basket full of berries on her back. Nayenezgani asked her where she came from and she replied: "I have been picking berries in the canyon, and there are many still there." Nayenezgani went on, and suddenly he saw the Bears coming towards him in single file. He immediately mounted his rainbow and rose into the air, and when he had gone up about fifteen feet, the Bears rushed under him trying to grasp his shadow. Nayenezgani then took his lightning arrows and killed them all.

The girl he had met on the way was a Bear in human form, and now she appeared coming up the canyon in her Bear form, and Nayenezgani killed her also. He then scalped the four Bears but not the Girl Bear. He dragged her down the canyon to a big piñon tree and spread her arms and legs far apart, put his head down close to hers, and said: "I will bring you back to life if you will promise not to harm people anymore." The Bear Maiden did not answer, but Nayenezgani blew four times on her head, and suddenly she came to life, sprang up, and ran away to the mountains. Then Nayenezgani went home and they celebrated as before.

After that, he asked his mother if there were any more monsters to be killed, and she answered: "No, you have killed them all. There are no more left." Nayenezgani was not sure that this was true, so he started out and visited all the mountains in the east looking for monsters, but he found none, and after that, he went to the mountains of the south, west, and north but found no more monsters to kill, so he came home again.

One evening after this, while sitting outside his hogahn, he saw a great red light to the north, and this made him angry, and he said to the people: "You said there were no more monsters to kill but there must be some over there." And he brought the people out of the hogahn, and they all saw the red light. Nayenezgani then took a forked stick, and stuck it in the ground, and aimed it at the fire so that, in the morning, he would be able to tell where the fire was. The next day, he looked along the stick and marked the place on the distant mountain to which the stick pointed before starting out, and then he mounted his rainbow and went there.

The place where the fire had been was at the La Plata River, and Nayenezgani found there an old woman, Sahn, who was Old Age. She was sleeping near a fire, while on the other side of the fire slept a black man, Bi-eth, which means Lazy Man or Sleepy-Man-of-No-Account. Nayenezgani raised his stone knife to kill the woman, but as he did so, he fell asleep and dropped down on the ground next to her.

The old woman woke up when he fell and said: "What is the matter, why do you try to kill me, Grandson?" And then she woke up Nayenezgani. Other people now came towards them. They were

Yah (Body Lice), Dechin (Hunger), Tayen (Thinness), and Ahtsaylin (Lies). Old Age begged Nayenezgani to spare her; she said she would hurt no one and that some people would love to be as old as she was. Bi-eth, or Sleepiness, also begged Nayenezgani not to kill him, as sleep is always good for people.

Yah, Body Lice, also begged for mercy and said: "I am good-natured, let me go."

Tayen, Thinness, begged for his life and said: "Thinness usually hurts no one."

Dechin, Hunger, begged for mercy, saying: "If you starve a little, you enjoy your food much more afterwards."

So Nayenezgani let them all go free, and he told the four—Hunger, Lice, Thinness, and Sleepiness—to go and stay at Tseh-dokohe, nine miles north of Farmington; and Old Age and Lies were to go to a place fifteen miles east of Pueblo Bonito, named Yath-pai. Then Nayenezgani went home again as there were some Yehtso-lapai (Grey Giants) wandering about. And Nayenezgani surrounded them, and left them at the spring of Tchah-toh near Huerfano, and turned them into stones.

Begochiddy came down again from heaven, and they told him about the killing of the monsters and he was very glad and said to them: "I will be back in twelve days, and we will have a Council."

Plans for Flood and Recreation

At the end of twelve days, Hashjeshjin (the Fire God) and all the gods came, and they held a Council in the Hogahn called Hadahonesteen (Mirage). The twins sat on one side of the Hogahn, and the gods on the other, and the gods talked very softly as they did not want the twins to hear them. They were talking of making more mountains and of fastening the mountains together with metal nails. The boys grew tired of hearing the whispering of the gods and wanted to know what they were talking about, and asked them to talk out loud so that they could hear. Their mother said to them: "We were talking of strengthening the mountains and putting them in good condition, and we are planning another flood to wash away all the old plants and trees, and of planting new ones, and of fastening the mountains down with metal, so that they will not be washed away in the flood." She said that the gods were glad that the bad monsters were killed and that they wanted to cleanse and recreate the world, and the twins agreed that this should be done.

So they began to fasten the mountains down with lead, gold, and so forth. And they worked seven days strengthening the mountains. Each mountain was strengthened and made in small size, but when Begochiddy used the Ethkaynah-ashi and blew at the mountains four times, they grew bigger and better than they were before. Then they killed all the trees because they thought them bad, and Begochiddy said that after seven days it would begin to rain. And all the gods went into the big bamboo flute again.

And the rain began and kept on for forty-two days, and water covered the whole earth except the tops of the mountains. When it stopped, a great rainbow appeared over the world, and on top of it stood Begochiddy with his hands spread out in gladness.

The water covered the world for forty-two days, and then began to decrease and run off in different directions, leaving only mountains and rocks and no plants or animals. The gods came back to Huerfano Peak where they had lived before, and Begochiddy waved his hands over the world, and at once, it was covered with trees and plants and animals, and when it had rained a little, everything began to grow. The gods planted a little cornfield called Dahgejol-gishy at Huerfano. They also grew their squash, beans, and tobacco there. They named the mountains again and also named some other places, Bezh-lachee-begizh—Washington Pass over the Chuskai Mountains; Tseh-hatral—volcanic rocks near the foot of the pass over the Chuskai Mountains; also Sontso-lah Mountain which is near Crystal, New Mexico; Tsen-tyel—Flat Rock in Canyon de Chelly; also Nashjeh-tseel—Spider Mountain or Peaked Rock in Canyon de Chelly; Toh-deh-hashkeh—on top of Black Mountain near Chin Lee; Ahdah-tintsoi—peak on Black Mountain; Nah-tee-tseel—Tobacco Mountain near Bluff City; Tsilth-kay-hozhoni—Beautiful Mountain north of Chuskai Mountain; Ahgeh-naschini—Crown Point; Tsis-kit—Cedar-Covered Flat-Topped Rock near Ojo Alamo. They visited these places as they named them and then went back to Huerfano.

Then they met again in the Hogahn for a Council with the boys sitting on one side and the gods on the other as before. And as before, the twins could not hear and asked after a time what the gods were talking about. Their mother said: "We are planning to make more people to fill this fine new world," and the boys were very glad to hear this. They discussed how the people were to be made and decided to make the men of turquoise and white corn, and the women of white shell and yellow corn, and the corn pollen would be for the male, and the corn bug for the female. The gods took these six things and turned them into three men and three women.

Begochiddy said: "I am going to a place called Siss-nah-tyel, which is near Kim-beto where Kay-des-tizhi, the Man-Wrapped-in-a-Rainbow lives. And I am going to plan to make animals there, and I shall make the donkey first, Tahilth-sapai, which means Dusty Beast because he is always rolling in ashes, then the sheep, then the horses, and after that, all sorts of animals." And Begochiddy laughed as he was planning these animals, and he kept going back and forth between Siss-nah-jini, which was his home, and the Council.

Creation of Man and Animals

Then they began to make Man. They made his feet, and his toenails, and his ankles of soil of the Earth, his legs of lightning, his knees of white shell, and his body of white corn and yellow corn. His veins were of striped corn and blue corn, the calico corn made the hair on his arms and body, the black corn made his eyebrows, and the red corn was his blood. His heart was of obsidian, and his breath was the white wind; his ear was made of white shell and the eardrum of mica. They took all the flesh of all the different animals to make his body, and also all other kinds of flower pollen. They made him of all kinds of water: rains, springs, lakes, rivers, and ponds, also of the black cloud and the male rain, and the sky, and the female rain, and they made his arms of the rainbow. His hair was made of darkness, his skull of the sun, his whiskers of darkness, and his face of daybreak. His nose was made of Yoh-lachee (red beads), his eyes of the Suns, his teeth of white corn, and his speech of thunder, his tongue of straight lightning, and the little whirlwind was what kept his nerves moving. The movement of his finger was the air, his saliva was the little rain, and the water of his nose and his tears were the medium rain; and his food was of white and yellow corn. And the name of the new kind of human being was Anlthtahn-nah-olyah, meaning Created-from-Everything. The people who had been in the cave were called Hahjeenah-dinneh, which means The-People-Who-Came-Up.

Hashje-altye (Talking God) was the first to be made, then Hashje-hogahn (House God), next Nahtahn-lakai-eshki (White Corn Boy), then Nahtahn-tsoi-atehd (Yellow Corn Girl), then Tradadeen-eshki (Corn Pollen Boy), then Tradadeen-atehd (Corn Pollen Girl), Sahanahray-eshki (the Holy Spirit Boy), and Bikay-hozhon-atehd (Holy Spirit Girl). These were the first human beings made on this earth of the substance of the universe which already was full of the Holy Spirit.

They made animals, and the donkey was made first of a substance called Ne-ho-pah, and his hoofs were made of obsidian.

This is the way they made men and creatures: they put everything which was used to make man laid out in pairs in a line on the Robe of Daybreak at the south, west, and north sides of the Hogahn and covered them with a buckskin. And the pair on the north side was covered with a rainbow as well as a buckskin. At the east side were the Yeh gods. The spirit of Siss-nah-jini Mountain motioned with a rainbow over all the human beings, and the Spirit of Tsoll-tsilth Mountain motioned over them with the sunlight, and they sang all night over the people and blessed them with the light and the rainbow, and towards daybreak, they took medicine and herbs and sprinkled over the human beings, and then the Yeh motioned over them with the Ethkaynah-ashi, and power came to them, and they were shaken with it.

The gods gave strong power to the people and covered them with flowers. And also they covered the new animals with plants and grasses; and then all the gods spoke and told the people four times to rise, that day had come. Then the Yeh took off the buckskins which had covered the people and the animals and Hashje-hogahn, the house God, gave his cry: Ah-ho-ah-ho. And the Yehs' spirits went in the four directions into the four Holy Mountains, and when the spirits entered the north mountain, the bird spirits went with them. The four mountains were called Siss-nah-jini, Tsoll-tsilth, Do-go-slee-ed, and Debeh-entsah. If people do not believe that the Yeh spirits are in these mountains and keep them holy, sickness and disease will come to afflict the people, for the Yehs control sickness (and that is the reason why the Indians are not healthy now, because at the ceremonies they do not take these things seriously).

Then the newly made people, Anlthtahn-nah-olyah, arose, and the gods motioned towards them with the Ethkay-nah-ashi and the new people spoke, saying: "Shemah (mother), Lecheh (father)," for they saw Begochiddy and called him father, and they called Estsan-ah-tlehay their mother. Then the new people ate some white corn, for, although they were made of corn, it was good for them to eat it, and the Navajos live on corn today.

First Song of the Hogahn

This ends the creating of human beings and creatures, and Begochiddy was glad and laughing when he had finished the creation.[6] And he made the new people run races around the world, and the animals raced too, and the donkey won, for Begochiddy loved him most, and the mule came in second. They then made a hogahn for the new people, and at present the hogahn song, Hogahn-beyin, is sung just after sundown for thanksgiving and as a prayer. Natah-hogahn-beyin is said.

After this, Begochiddy turned all the animals loose to wander as they pleased, but the donkey was kept for his own use; and he said to the animals: "Some day I will come back and need you, but now you can wander as you please." There were a great many songs sung while he was making the animals, and there are so many of these songs that today very often not all of the songs are sung in one night's ceremony.

They gathered for another Council in the Hogahn, and again the gods spoke so low that Nayenezgani and his brother, Tohbachischin, could not hear what they said, and the twins asked the gods to speak so that they could understand them and the gods answered: "We were talking about the creating of animals and human beings, and how you killed the monsters. Now we are planning to go and get the people (Hahjeenah-dinneh) who are living in the cave."

Nayenezgani said: "That is well."

Then they made a great rainbow shaped like a basin, and they all mounted this and went to the cave. They asked Nayenezgani and his brother to go, but Etsay-hashkeh, the Coyote, stayed behind as he did not care to go, and the other gods did not urge him.

While the gods were gone on the journey to the cave, the Coyote made some little coyotes of his own, a white one from the east, a yellow one from the west, which was a female, a blue one from the south, which was a male, and a black coyote from the north, which was a female, and each pair stood nose to nose; and he also made a dog, which stood with the female black coyote. The names of these coyotes were: the east, Ki-othkath-tee-ni-gosai, which means Turning-in-the-Daybreak; west, Nahotsoi-nah-go-sai, which means Turning-in-the-Afterglow; south, Chadidoth-dani-gosai, which means Turning-in-the-Darkness; and the name of the dog was Dobinny-des-daha, or Trailing Dog. Etsay-hashkeh also made some crazy coyotes. If one of these should bite a human being, he would probably go mad. And also he made some mad dogs whose bites would bring madness.

Etsay-hashkeh made these creatures because he did not know how to behave, and no one was there to know what he was doing. And though Begochiddy knew what the Coyote was doing, he was willing that these animals should be made.

Notes

1. The Black God sand painting of the Tleji or Yehbechai ceremony has to do with this part of the story.
2. The sand painting of the place of emergence has to do with this part of the story.
3. Female and male, respectively.
4. This was the first mother-in-law trouble.
5. Hasteen Klah noted that from this point present-day Navajos know the story.
6. Hasteen Klah said. "The only two people who know the Creation Song today are Nakai-John (Klah's older brother) and myself." Klah died in 1936.

Origin of the Two-Spirits

Destruction of the Kia´nakwe... (1904)

(Zuñi)

Recorder: Matilda Coxe Stevenson

The day was still young when these gods requested Kŏw´wituma, Wats´uusi, a man of the Coyote clan, and To´na O´ᵗsi (Turkey man[1]) to muster about a pottery drum and dance. The man of the Coyote clan was provided with a drumstick, such as is used at the present time for these drums. U´yuyewi, Maᵗsai´lema, all those who had participated in fighting, and the Ashiwanni joined in the broken circle around the group, each man in the circle having a woman of his paternal clan by his side.

By command of Kŏw´wituma, the man of the Coyote clan gave four loud and distinct strokes upon the drum and then beat it rapidly, which called forth seven beings from the depths of the earth, who took their places in the group. The circle moved slowly, with even, measured step. Those in the circle sang, Kŏw´wituma, keeper of the songs, leading the song. After four songs, or stanzas, the To´na O´ᵗsi struck the drum with his great claws four times, each time clearly and with great force. Each stroke caused the hearts of the enemy to tremble and jump with fear. He then beat rapidly upon the drum while those forming the circle sang four songs, after which the A´shiwi, accompanied by the Divine Ones, U´yuyewi and Maᵗsai'lema, advanced to meet the enemy, who were discovered to be the Kia´nakwe, though the A´shiwi called them the white people, because they all wore mi´has.[2]

The fighting continued four days. The Kia´nakwe were compelled to close their nostrils with raw cotton to avoid the sulfurous odors emitted from the bodies of the A´shiwi. At night, each party fell back: the Kia´nakwe to their village and the A´shiwi to Hän´ᵗlipinkia, where they danced and prayed throughout the night for rain.

The second night, the Kia´kwemosi sent the Divine Ones to Ko´thluwala´wa to inquire if A´wan tä´^{t}chu Ko´yemshi could tell anything about the enemy and to implore the Council of the Gods to cause rainfall, that the A´shiwi bowstrings, which were made of yucca fiber, might be made strong and the bowstrings of the enemy, made of deer sinew, might be weakened. The A´shiwis secured their arrows for the engagement with the Kia´nakwe on Ko´yemshi Mountain.[3]

The prayers of the A´shiwi brought heavy rains on the third morning, and again, they met the enemy. This time, their forces were strengthened by the Kok´ko, present at the request of U´yuyewi and Ma^{t}sai´lema, who were now the recognized Gods of War. Again Ku´yapäli^{t}sa, the ^{t}Cha´kwena, walked in front of her army, shaking her rattle. She succeeded in capturing four of the gods from Ko´thluwala´wa—Kor´kokshi, the first born of Si´wulutsiwa and Si´wulu^{t}si^{t}sa; It´^{t}sepäsha (game-maker), one of the nine last-born; a Sa´ya^{t}hlia (blue horn, a warrior god); and a Sha´läko (one of the couriers to the uwannami (rain-makers). These gods succeeded in making their escape, but all were captured except the Sha´läko, who ran so like a hare that he could not be caught.

The Kia´nakwe had a dance in which the prisoner gods appeared in celebration of their capture. Kor´kokshi, the firstborn, was so angry and unmanageable that Ku´yapäli^{t}sa had him dressed in female attire previous to the dance, saying to him: "You will now perhaps be less angry."[4]

Notes

1. This personage was a turkey of enormous size.
2. These are white, cotton, embroidered blankets. The Zuñis say they never saw the mi´ha until they met the Kia´nakwe, but they afterward wove it of their native cotton. The modern mi´ha is made by the Hopi priests and consists of commercial cotton in the body of the blanket and wools for embroidery. They are exclusively ceremonial and are the most valued of all fabrics known to

these people. The principal designs in the embroidery are conventional butterflies and cloud and lightning symbols.

3. Ko´yemshi Mountain, in the immediate vicinity of Ko´thluwala´wa, was found to have been a central place for arrow making.
4. The Zuñis assert this to be the first instance of a god or man appearing in woman's dress.

The First Alyha (1972)

(Mohave)

Narrator: Nyavarup

Recorder: A.L. Kroeber

It was inside the house at Avikwame.[1] Four women were sitting near Mastamho.[2] He said to the one at the southeast (center post), to Hatšinye-(nya)-masām-arītše: "You are the one who will be a doctor, I think."

Then he said to the one sitting at the northeast, to Hatšinye-(nya)masām-hiwāim: "You are the one who will not listen to what your kin say to you; you will be loose." And to Umas-erau, a man sitting to the southwest, he said: "And you are the one who will have intercourse with her!" Umas-erau did not answer.

Now two other women were sitting there: Hatšinye-kwatpārve at the northwest, and Hatšinye-kwatš'iδe[3] at the southwest.[4] Hatšinye-kwatpārve was about to have a baby, and Hatšinye-kwatš'iδe was going to receive it and held out her left hand. But Mastamho said: "No, take it with your right hand:[5] that will be good. Now lay the child's head to the north, not to the south![6] Then it will dream well; if it lies to the south, it will dream badly."[7]

Now the baby lay there, looking around. "Sit back from him there," Mastamho said. "That boy knows much more than you all: he will be a leader."

The baby was looking this way and that, its eyes winking. Then it said: "I want a name. What will you call me?"

Mastamho said: "He is a boy, but I think we will give him not a boy's name, nor a man's, but a girl's. I call him Hatšinye-hai-kwatš'iδe."[8]

Mastamho picked up the baby, held it in his hands. "I will tell you all about him. I want you to learn what I will teach about this child." Then he sang, swaying his hands from side to side with the child on them, and the four women[9] danced to his motions.

When he laid the child down, the boy thought: "I am a boy; but shall I wear a breech-clout or not? Shall I wear girl's clothes or boy's?"

I[10] was there. I saw it; I heard Mastamho singing. I did not sing then, but I know how to.

Now the boy was old enough to play about. There was no iδo, black willow, yet in existence, so Mastamho created it, to make a bow from. Then he gave it to him. Carrying his bow, the boy went outdoors to where little girls were playing, but he did not keep the bow. First he held it behind his back, then, looking around to see if he was unobserved, he threw it away.

When the little girls came indoors, Mastamho asked them: "Did the boy keep his bow?"

One of them answered: "He had no bow." He had been ashamed to tell them of it.

Then Mastamho made him another. "Perhaps he did not like that one; perhaps he will like a different one." He split black willow, made a bow, feathered arrows, and gave them to him. Then the boy went outdoors; he went into a group of girls. He walked four steps and let his bow fall to the ground.

They said to him: "Pick up your bow and arrow," but he did not answer. Then one of them, Hatšinye-masām-kuvetškie,[11] went over, picked it up, and held it out to him. But he only looked at it; he would not take it.

They came indoors from their playing and Mastamho asked: "How about the boy?"

A girl said: "He threw it away; I have it!"

"Yes?" said Mastamho, "he did not keep it?"

"Yes, he did not keep it," she said.

Mastamho thought: "I think it did not suit him. I will make him a different one. I will scrape it fine and white and put a feather on it, and another, and another." So he gave the boy a pretty bow and arrow.

The boy went outside, took four steps northwest of the house, threw down his bow and arrow where a group of girls had sat down to make dolls.[12] They said to him: "We will make you a doll." They did not look him in the face but said softly to one another: "I think the boy is going to be [a] girl: he wants a doll."

He said: "I do not want a doll; I know how to make it for myself." He would not take the one they offered him. He held his hands in front of him and moved them slowly in jerks[13] sidewise and out and back, singing[14] softly inside of himself.

The girls said to one another: "Don't look at him, don't look at him, or he will be ashamed and not play with dolls anymore."

When they had played, they started to go indoors again. "Here, take your bow," a girl said and handed it to him. He did not take hold of it right, by the grip in the middle, but dangling from the string, and followed them in. "Look at him," they thought, "he is not doing the right way. He is going to become a girl."

Mastamho asked them: "How did he do this time? Has he his bow?"

They said: "No, when he arrived, he threw it northwest.[15] He did not take care of it but got a doll and sat like a girl,[16] with the doll lying across his thighs."

"Then what did he do?"

"I don't know; he played with his doll, the same as we."

So Mastamho called the boy to him. "Give me your hand," he said. "First we called you Hatšinye-kwatpārve.[17] But that will not be your name any longer. You will be called Hatšinye-tomeŝike. Now you may go with these girls."

Then Mastamho made a set of stave-dice[18] out of his breath and spittle and handed them to the boy. "I give you this." The boy seized them, held them tight so as not to lose them, tucked them away.[19] Mastamho said: "Come on outdoors. Let us try whether this boy will play dice like a girl. But do not turn to the east[20]—who goes that way will be a doctor. Go by the right hand, then it will be well." So all stood about to see whether the boy would play like a girl.

A woman was sitting at the southwest, laughing; the boy sat on the northeast (facing her). He took the dice to throw them with his left hand; she said: "No, throw them with the right!" When he threw them up, she was opposite, struck them in mid-air, and scattered them.[21] Then everyone laughed and there was a big noise. And the boy too laughed like a woman now, and smiled like one. Then the woman threw the staves up and he struck them down, and again all laughed. As they started again to play (the third time), all the girls who had been sitting rose to kneel to see better; and the boy threw.

When the woman was to throw for the fourth play, Mastamho called: "Stand up, everybody! Are you all standing?" When they said: "Yes," the woman threw, the boy caught them in his hand, and all laughed; one could hear it far off. Now the boy had it: he knew all that the girls knew.

Mastamho said: "When I made these (dice), I gave them to this boy, and now he has them. Now all you women and girls[22] come close by me; I will tell you. That boy will stand in front; he will be the head one." Then Mastamho sang: "Histūm!" ("He has it!"). Then he said to him: "Now you have it. And your name will be Hatšinye-tomeδīke."

Two women were laughing: they wanted the boy to laugh like themselves. Then he laughed like that. "Now you laugh like a woman," they said.

Then Mastamho went over to all the girls to sing, and stood to the southwest, the boy facing him from the northeast[23] and listening to him. And after Mastamho had said it four times, the boy sang: "A'avek" ("I hear it"). Then he danced, first to the west, then to the south, north, east,[24] four times.

Now Mastamho made a dress out of his body[25] and handed it to the boy. "Nyā'áim nyahvai," "I give you the dress," he said. So the boy put it on, the thick wide apron piece behind, the narrow one in front. "Now walk," said Mastamho, "so we can see how you look moving." So the boy took four steps, then turned and faced him. Mastamho asked him: "Now you have heard what I told the women about how to dress and behave. Do you understand that?"

The boy said, "Yes," nodding his head.

The alyha can cure sexual disease. Alyha is also the name for gonorrhea. That is why the Indians had that sickness: Mastamho gave it to them, and these alyha were to cure it. Syphilis and blue scrotum came from the whites,[26] gonorrhea they had before.[27]

Mastamho said: "We will sing and see how you dance." So he sang, and all the women danced on the east, the boy standing dancing alone on the west. Mastamho wanted to lead them outdoors[28]; he was singing, they following him dancing. When they were all out, Mastamho asked Hatšinye-tomeδīke "Do you understand what I have taught you?"

"Yes, I heard it, I know it."

"Well, let me see you do it then."

So the boy stood facing west, with Mastamho behind him, and talked to all the women opposite. Then they all together answered "ê" with a loud noise.

Mastamho walked about behind the boy, listening whether he said everything right. He had said: "You can do it; you know how, I will not tell you more." So the boy was telling the women and girls what to do, and they took one another's hands and listened to him.

He said: "Hatšinye-masām-kwatšārve kinneik," "All you girls (and people)[29] approach." Then he sang and danced and they danced with him.

Mastamho had told him: "When you dance, walk backward and make them follow you (forward)." So he walked backward toward Mastamho, singing, and Mastamho backed too, and all the others followed them. He sang loudly, and they all sang with him, and as he sang he blew saliva on them, white spots, as if they were painted.[30]

When they finished singing, Mastamho spoke again. "I ordain[31] that some women when married will be quiet, and good workers. And some will not stay with their husbands but be loose. And some will be doctors, but not marry." That is why there are few women doctors. "Well, we are all here.[32] Let us go south. After four steps,[33] I will arrange a place; I will call it Miakwa'orve.[34] That is where we will stop and do something." So they all came to Miakwa'orve. There Mastamho said: "I call you all Hatšinye-masām-mitšovθe;"[35] and all the women danced as he talked to them.

Notes

1. The scene is to be visualized as follows. It is in the great house at Avikwame, with four center posts, and the door as always to the south (leeward). Mastamho is sitting just outside the square of center posts, off the southwest one (right front, as one looks from inside toward the door). The four women sit inside the square, each by a post, their order of mention being SE, NE, NW, SW—a counterclockwise circuit. The baby when born is laid in the middle of the central square. This precision of visualization is characteristic of the

Mohave, and among themselves they mostly seem to think it important enough to describe. My notes contain a diagram. Unfortunately, I failed to set down whether the diagram was scratched in the sand for me by the narrator (or interpreter), or was constructed by myself from their verbal explanation. However, the omission bears only on the question of how far the Mohave have impulses to give their dream visualizations kinesthetic conversion; the spatial organization of the visual imaginings is evident.

2. Mastamho called himself Pahutsats-yamasam-kyuvetski. There was a woman there (beyond the four mentioned) whom he called Hatsinye-masam-kupawa. She answered, "Yes, that is my name." (She did and said nothing else.)
3. Or -kuvatš'iБe.
4. Completing the anti-sunwise circuit, begun at the SE.
5. The left hand is for doctoring.
6. The dead go S from Mohave land.
7. Be unlucky, die soon.
8. The same name as the midwife's, except for the element -hai-.
9. The doctor woman, the promiscuous woman, the mother, and the midwife.
10. The narrator, Nyavarup.
11. It is not clear why she should be singled out for mention by name.
12. Dolls may be of rude pottery, or perhaps of bast or rags.
13. Why the jerky motion? He is probably making his doll. The narrator illustrated with gestures, keeping time to a song.
14. The words of the alyha's song were given as: "Idauk ilyuvik," "I hold it, it is finished." These recur in the songs of paragraph 31: the range of vocabulary in most Mohave songs seems to be remarkably limited and monotonous. See the examples in Raven, 4, notes 4, 8, 11, 13, 24, 31 (UC-AR 11:1) 38, 39, 40; Deer, 5 (UC-AR 11:1) 42; in *Handbook*, 757, 758, 763, 776; and *passim* below.
15. This type of specification is characteristic. It would not matter to us what the direction was, nor would it matter in the tales of most primitive peoples. But the Mohave insist on being ritual-mannered in their myths; perhaps because they have so little formal ritual. Or it might be better to say that their myths *are* rituals—narrated, unperformed ceremonies. Certainly song-series like theirs usually are part of rituals. (NW would be behind the house to the left, as one faces the door.)
16. Mohave women about 1902 sat with their legs stretched out, perhaps crossed at the ankles; or with one leg doubled under, the other either stretched out on the ground or with the knee up; or with legs folded over, Turk or tailor fashion. Men, on the contrary, sat on their legs both turned on the same side, or with their heels directly under them, thighs straight forward; both these being usual women's positions in the Plains, Plateau, and California. This is according to my observations as noted down.
17. His mother's name in 3. There may have been an error in understanding or translation.
18. Otaha. Four staves or billets of willow or similar wood (*Handbook* 741). One side is painted red and blue, generally perhaps with three different designs on the four pieces, but the variation of pattern does not enter into the scoring.

The count is: all four plain sides up, 2 points; all four painted, 1; any mixed combination, O.

19. Presumably in the band of his shirt—which, however, he did not yet have on.
20. East is to the left, coming out the door.
21. This is how the game is played: one throws them up close together, the other beats them down to scatter.
22. A girl, masahai, has not yet borne a child; she may be virgin or married. A woman, θenya'aka, is a matron, however youthful.
23. With his back to the house.
24. Not a circuit this time: W, S, N, E.
25. By reaching into it and taking out what he wanted.
26. Wherever in California I have had statements from Indians on the source of syphilis, it was credited to the whites. The only statement I have recorded which is possible indirect evidence of gonorrhea in native times is a northwest California Karok tale in which the lecherous culture hero and trickster blinds his grandson by rubbing semen over his eyes.
27. This paragraph is a digression from the myth.
28. They have got indoors again, without explicit mention in the narrative.
29. "Men and women"—although hatsinye refers to little girls.
30. Having saliva froth blown on them is something the Mohave accept with indifference: it is standard in the process of being cured by shamans. It is of a piece with other customs; such as ribaldry as regards sex; cooking fish into stew with scales, bones, and perhaps entrails left in; one person after another sucking the sugar out of the same mass of mesquite meal. They are not a squeamish people. And this in turn is part of their pride in enduring discomfort and hardship cheerfully.
31. "We appoint it," the interpreter said.
32. Men as well as women.
33. These steps are magically long: the distance is a number of miles.
34. For Miakwa'orve see "A," west side, on Map I and (UC-AR 11:2), 140. In the early historic period it seems to have been the uppermost permanent large settlement in Mohave Valley. It is where Nyohaiva originated, in 3:1 (UCAR 11:1), 28. Here, "Amiakwa'orve" was heard; once I wrote "Imiakwa'orve"; the initial vowel is slurred, the word accent is on the *a* before *k*, and again on the *o*.
35. Again, men as well as women appear to be included, cf. fn. 22 above.

[The First Hwami] (1972)

(Mohave)

Narrator: Nyavarup

Recorder: A. L. Kroeber

Mastamho was singing.[1] He called a girl Hatšinye-masam-merīke.[2] He said to her: "Listen!"

She said: "Yes, I hear."

Mastamho said: "If you hear all that I sing, do you know it?"

She said: "Yes."

Then he said: "Let me hear you sing it."

Then she sang; she sang to him: "Vanālye,[3] stand back!" She sang what he had sung.

Then he said: "Yes, now you have it. It is good. You have not lost a word."

She was the first Hwami.[4]

Notes

1. This paragraph is certainly in answer to an inquiry about how transvestites came to be.
2. Meaning of term unknown.
3. Meaning unknown.
4. Hwami are the rare women leading men's lives; the male alyha are not accounted for here. [See "The First Alyha" in this volume. —JE]

How Lizard Sodomized Coyote (1984)

(Chemehuevi)

Narrator: George Laird

Recorder: Carobeth Laird

While Coyote was going along, he heard a shrill whistle (that sounded like), "Oh, Coyote, come over and anus-fuck me!"

"Haiky*a*! Who is it that wants me to come and anus-fuck him—aiky*a*?" Saying thus, Coyote was looking all around. Then he found Lizard (Sigɨpits*ɨ*).

"What did you say—aiky*a*?"

"'Oh, Coyote, I am going to anus-fuck you!' thus I said."

"No—aiky*a*! 'Oh, Coyote, come over and anus-fuck me!' That is what you said—aiky*a*!"

"I did not. 'Coyote, I am going to anus-fuck you,' that is what I said."

"No—aiky*a*! I am going to do it to you first—aiky*a*!"

"No, I am going to do it to you first; I said it first."

Then Lizard did it to Coyote. When he got through, he ran away and entered into a crack in a rock.

"Haiky*a*! Come out—aiky*a*! I am going to do it to you too—aiky*a*!"

When Lizard did not come out, Coyote began to jab at him, poking a stick into the crack.

From inside the crack Lizard sang:

The sky will fall
if I die, if I die.
The sky will fall
if I die, if I die.

Thus said Lizard.

"Haiky*a*! What are you saying—aiky*a*, that the sky would fall—aiky*a* if you should die—aiky*a*?" Saying this, Coyote began to poke him again.

Then the sky made a cracking sound.

"Haiky*a*! It seems that you told the truth— aiky*a*! That being so, you may live—aiky*a*!"

Red-Woman and Old-Man-Coyote's Wife (1918)

(Crow)

Recorder: Robert H. Lowie

Red-woman[1] said, "Just as soon as the skin of buffalo is taken off, it shall be soft and ready to use."

Old-Man-Coyote's wife said, "It will be better to have to work on it." From that time on they have to work on their hides.

Red-woman said, "I'd like to build a fire once, and that fire shall go forever."

Old-Man-Coyote's wife said, "I don't like it that way. I want to put in several kinds of work, getting firewood and building the fire."

Red-woman said, "I'll make it so we can take grease right out of a buffalo."

Old-Man-Coyote's wife said, "I don't want it that way, I want some work on it." So since then they have to work to get the grease.

Red-woman said, "When we're born we'll live for forty years."

Old-Man-Coyote's wife said, "I don't want it that way. People shall die any time before that." Since then children grow sick and die.

Red-woman said, "When a person dies, we shall bury the body and let that be the end of it."

Old-Man-Coyote's wife said, "I'd like to have people cry and cut their fingers and legs and heads when someone dies, also go for a vision." Since then they have done thus.

Red-woman said, "I'll make a dead body get up again in four days."

"Someone else has to take care of the souls."[2]

Red-woman wanted to make it summer all the time. Old-Man-Coyote's wife said, "I'd like to go on ice. I want winter." Since then we have had winter.

Red-woman said, "Early in the spring, grass and leaves will come up together; when the leaves get big enough, they'll change color and fall to the ground to make good soil for the earth so as to come up again next year."

Red-woman wanted no air, and Old-Man-Coyote's wife said, "I want air. It's one of the things I like best. If there is no air, we can't breathe." Since then we have had air.

Red-woman wanted to make one river across the land. "I want several rivers, so they can get a drink anywhere."

Old-Man-Coyote's wife said, "I want water to run in coulées and to have trees and brush grow all over so we can get wood and build a fire in any place."

Red-woman said, "I'll plant grass all over the road and there shall be nothing but grass."

"No, flowers and other plants shall grow too, so that if anyone is sick they can get roots for medicine."

Old-Man-Coyote's wife said, "Make all kinds of fruit to grow among the trees, also strawberries among the grass, they'll keep us from starving."

Red-woman said, "What about the cherries?"

Old-Man-Coyote's wife replied, "We'll make it so that the sun ripens fruit, we'll make it black when it is ripe. We'll be able to tell thus when they are ripe."

"After skinning a buffalo," Red-woman asked, "how are you going to fix it up?"

Old-Man-Coyote's wife answered: "We'll get the brains of the buffalo and prairie plants with grease, also liver, to turn it into a soft hide." Since then these were used to soften the hide.

Old-Man-Coyote's wife said, "I have forgotten something."

Red-woman said, "You have not forgotten anything." Red-woman wanted all men and women to be all of the same size and to run all the same way and be all the same way.

"That way you'll have lots of trouble. We'll give women a dress and leggings to be tied above the knee so they can't run, and they shall not be as strong as men." That is why men are stronger than women. They made a mistake with some, who became half-men and since then we have had bāté (berdaches).

Red-woman said, "We forgot to give people any medicines. What shall they be?"

"Give wishes to the Indians and also presents to the Sun and sweat lodge and Tobacco (í ʻtsiʻtsī̂ *a*)."

Old-Man-Coyote's wife said, "What will you do with people going out for visions?"

"When their tears fall on the ground, they'll get pay for it some day and some day they'll live well." Since then anyone going out on a vision lives well and sometimes they find plenty of horses.

Old-Man-Coyote's wife said, "What shall you do about horses?"

"They'll get old and die any time." Since then horses die any time, some of them when old.

Old-Man-Coyote's wife asked, "What about buffalo?"

"I'll fix it so that people can butcher them and know where to cut so they can butcher easily. There shall be no joints in the arms, so there will be an easy butchering."

Old-Man-Coyote's wife asked, "With what shall people kill buffaloes?"

"There is plenty of material in the world to kill with. Use chokecherry trees for arrows and stones for arrowheads."

Old-Man-Coyote's wife asked, "If no chokecherry trees are near, what then?"

"They can use any wood for arrows." Since then they have used any kind.

"What shall we use for bows?"

Red-woman said, "Sinew for the string and twist it." Since then sinew is used for bows.

Red-woman said, "Arrow points can be found in any place." That is why rocks are found all over the country.

Old-Man-Coyote's wife asked, "What are you going to do with the Crow Indians?"

"We'll put them in the middle of the other tribes. They can fight the rest of the tribes. They can have fun that way."

Notes

1. Doubtless meant to be identical with Hícictawîa.
2. Obscure.

Warrior Girl (1928)

(Tewa)

Recorder: Elsie Clews Parsons

Where they were living lived Pohaha, a girl[1] who would not mind her mother or father or uncle. They were telling her to be a good girl, but she got angry quickly. Then they got tired telling her to be good, so they just let her go.

One time she was grinding corn, and many enemies were coming, very close to the village. Her uncle came to her house and asked her mother where she was. Her mother said she was grinding corn.

He went to where she was grinding and caught her arm and said, "Take your bow and arrows and go and fight with the enemies who are coming. You would not mind us and behaved like a boy. Now is the time for you to go and fight and be brave," said the uncle to the girl.

She laughed *ha! ha!* "I am very glad to go," she said. "I am very anxious to go and fight the enemies. I am not afraid. I will do all I can."

"That is why I tell you. Come out!" said the uncle.

"I will," she said. She stood up and her uncle gave her bow and arrows and hung the bandolier around her.

Then she looked around and there was a rattle hanging on the wall. She stepped up and got it. Then she started to sing. As soon as she stopped singing, she laughed *ha! ha!* She sang four times in the room. Then she went out and sang outdoors four times. Whenever she paused in singing she laughed *ha! ha!* because she was not afraid to fight.

Then she started, and the men followed her. People were saying, "The Cottonwood People (clan) girl (*te' towa*) is going to fight."

Some of them laughed at her. But she just went on, singing and laughing *ha! ha!* happy she was going to fight.

Before she met the enemies, she pulled her dress up, four times, to show the enemies that she was a girl. Then she fought. She killed all the enemies that same day. After that, the fighting was over, and she turned back.

The men fighting with her saw she had turned *okuwa*. She was wearing a mask, one side was blue, and one side was yellow, and she had long teeth. They were afraid of her, she looked strange, she no longer looked like a girl. But she kept on singing her song, ending with *ha! ha!*

She kept on going home, and the men followed her. When they got to the village, all the people came out and watched the girl, how she had become some sort of a person. When she went to war, she did not look like that.

She went to her house and went in, and then she took off her mask and hung it on the wall, and she hung her rattle in the same place and the bow and arrow close, too. That is the way that girl became *pohaha*![2]

Her uncles came to the house at night. They had been talking about her. All day they had been thinking that she must be a man. So they went in there, all gathered together. The oldest uncle[3] said they would put her in as Pota'i (war chief). Even if she was a girl, she was a man, too.

So they said that whenever enemies came she was to be the leader in war. "You have to watch for the people," they told her. "If any sickness comes, you have to drive the sickness away from the people. And consider that the people are all your children. Treat them right," they told her.

After that, she became a good girl. She no longer acted as she used to. When war came, she went first and dressed as she did before in war.

After she died, she left her mask and said that it would represent her. She would always be with the people, even if dead. "I will be with you all the time," she said. "The mask is me," she said.

That is why those Cottonwood People keep that mask.

Notes

1. Chakwena *mui su'amö* (their grandmother) was similarly a girl, sent to war by her uncles, and also, while she was fighting, her face turned into a mask. Her mother was combing her hair, and had only one side whorled, and the stick she used was still in the whorl. Then her uncle came in. (The scene between Pohaha and her uncle is repeated.) In this case the uncle also gives a quiver of mountain lion skin and the mask is different, too, black, with yellow eyes, and tongue hanging out. The same story is told of He''e'e', whose mask is also black with yellow round eyes. Hair like that of Chakwena their grandmother, but crow tail feathers are at the back of the head. He''e'e' belongs to Powamu chief. (See Fewkes 2: Pls. IV, X1.)
2. Named from her call [*ha! ha!*—JE] and *po,* meaning wet. While she was fighting she was very wet between her legs. But compare term *powaka.*
3. The characteristic Hopi-Tewa maternal family is being referred to, the English term "uncle" always meaning in the mouth of a Pueblo Indian (Taos alone excepted) mother's brother or mother's mother's brother. The influence of the "uncle" comes out clearly in this tale, as well as the relation between maternal family and clan.

MEN WHO BECAME WOMEN

The Eight Young Men Who Became Women (1903)

(Comanche)

Narrator: Ridge-Bear

Recorders: George A. Dorsey and Alfred L. Kroeber

There was a party of eight young men on the warpath.[1] All were very good-looking. When they made a camp for the night, one of them turned into a female. When the other young men were roasting beef for themselves, this man, now a woman, was separate from her companions, on account of her sex, feeling ashamed. The first camp was made of light cottonwood trees. The rest of the young men did not know what ailed the disheartened one, but said, "If there is something the matter with you, you had better return home. If you think you would be comfortable there, it is to your advantage to go home." But this young woman never said a single word during a period of four days.

At the end of four days, she became a man again, the same as at first. The party was still proceeding on a journey. A second man turned into a woman, but kept it a secret, as the first one had done. The first one had not told his companions why he was separated from them without eating for four days, but observing that this man's actions were like his own, he knew what was the trouble with him. The second man, having gone without food for four days, became a man again.

Thus it happened with all of the party until the last one had gone through with the experience, when the first one to experience the happening told the rest he knew what was the trouble with them, for he was the first one to experience it. This transformation occupied a period of thirty-two days.

These young men did not want to return home, for they felt that they would rather die in battle than return to the tribe half woman and half man, so each made up his mind to remain on the journey and take his chance, for if they died of contracted disease, it would be better than to be known as half woman and half man.

These young men contracted the change of sex while camped under eight cottonwood trees. When they returned they at once told the people that a strange incident had occurred to them while on the warpath.

Note

1. Said to have been obtained by the Comanche.

The Hermaphrodite (1906)

(Pawnee)

Narrator: White-Sun

Recorder: George A. Dorsey

There was a village and in this village lived a fine-looking young man. The young man never cared anything for women, but one night a young girl came to his bed and they lay together. After they had lain together for a while, the young man sent the girl away.

He then went to a fine spring that was gushing forth from the side of a hill and took a bath. Then he went home and lay down. That night in a dream he saw Spider-Woman sitting with her legs spread out and a spring of water was coming out from between her legs. Spider-Woman told the boy in his dream that, as he had come and washed after having connection with the woman, from that time on he should be like a woman.

The boy woke up; he could not sleep anymore.

The next day, the dream worried him, and for several days, he felt as though he were sick, and he had a medicine man come and wait on him. The medicine man could not tell what was the matter.

One time they sent for one of the medicine men who, on examining him, told him that he was turning into a woman. The medicine man told the relatives of the young man that he was turning into a woman and that Spider-Woman was the cause of it, that the only way he could cure the young man was by having the relatives of the boy go to the creeks, springs, or any streams of water and get the green moss from the bottom of the streams and bring it to him.

The people went to the streams of water, but there was not any moss to be found. The medicine man said: "Spider-Woman knows that I can cure the young man if I can get this moss; she has caused all this moss to disappear, so I cannot cure him."

When the boy heard that the medicine men could not do anything for him, he was so ashamed that he committed suicide rather than be half woman and half man.[1]

Note

1. The common belief in the fact that springs take their origin from spider-women is emphasized in this tale. The teaching of the story is the warning given to young men not to bathe in springs after sexual intercourse—that is, while unclean. Not only must this be done for the good of the tribe, but also because the spider-woman, representing one of the supernatural earthly beings, must be treated with a certain amount of respect.

Mä'näbus Outwits Turtle (1915)

(Menomini)

Narrator: John V. Satterlee

Recorders: Alanson Skinner and John V. Satterlee

Mä'näbus was mourning for his little brother that had been killed. In those days people used to blacken their faces and wear their hair long to show their sorrow.

The Indians nearby were going to have a feast, and they invited Mä'näbus who prepared to go.

Now at that time, Mik´änâ, the turtle, was very powerful, so he and Mä'näbus were selected by the host to have the special privilege of eating the head of the bear.

When they got together and Mä'näbus told Turtle that he was chosen to eat with him, Turtle was disgusted, especially since Mä'näbus was scratching his head with a little stick.[1]

"You look like an old woman with your hair long and blackened face," said Turtle.

Mä'näbus was very angry, but said nothing, and the host asked them to hurry and choose two other men to make the quartet, who were to partake of the bear's head. When the feast was over, Mä'näbus went home, Turtle's insult rankling in his heart.

Now Turtle had a wonderful pair of medicine leggings with deer hoof rattles. "Ssh! Ssh! Ssh!" they went, as he walked, and he had a powerful robe all spotted like a fawn skin. It was in these two things that the secret of his magic lay.

"Änä´äämékût Mud Turtle!" ejaculated Mä'näbus to himself. "Everybody heard what you said to me. Even if you have those strong powers, I guess I can get ahead of you."

After a while, Mä'näbus hit upon a plan. "Let me be a nice, beautiful girl." No sooner said than done, and Mä'näbus looked in his mirror and was much pleased at his lovely appearance. "I am really too pretty for that fellow," he said, and he calmly took out one eye and laid it on a rock. "Oh my! I look too homely now," so he decided to put it back, but when he reached for it, it was gone, for Marten, who was passing that way, had run away with it. "Come back and give me my eye," shouted Mä'näbus. "I just left it there for a minute."

Back trotted the marten, obediently, and gave Mä'näbus the eye which he put in again.

Then Mä'näbus grabbed Marten. "Of course I'll take you with me," he said. "I am going to call on Turtle, and you can be my baby, and you have such a nice face." Then they started for Mud Turtle's.

Mud Turtle lived close to a village, and when Mä'näbus arrived, he purposely walked through it, passing by a group of young men. "My! what a lovely girl," they said as he passed by a large lodge.

He went in and asked if he might stay there. The people said he might and gave him a place. In the evening as he sat by the fire all the young men came in and peeped at him in admiration.

At last all the family retired, Mä'näbus with the rest. The young men were talking to each other outside. At last one bolder than the rest said he would go in and see the girl, so he crawled in cautiously.

"Who are you?" asked Mä'näbus, and the young fellow told him, explaining that he had seen him go by and had been inspired to come in and pay a call. Mä'näbus acted very sweetly. "Oh the reason why I came here is that I want to see Mud Turtle. Won't you do me the favor to go and call him." The man tried hard to find out why she wanted to see Turtle. "Oh, I just want to see him because I have heard that he is more powerful than all the other men. I am poor and I live all alone and I want to see him."

The young man could get no further information, so at last he slipped out to those who were waiting breathlessly to learn the outcome of his visit. "How did you get along?" they asked.

"Oh, I had poor luck for she is crazy to see Mud Turtle, and she begged me to call him."

"Don't do it. You must not," they entreated. "Let somebody else try."

Then another young man went in, but he went through the same experience.

"Where is that first young man?" asked Mä'näbus.

"He is still out there," said the visitor.

"Why I asked him to call Mud Turtle."

"Oh!" said the other, "he has not gone. He is right there, the other men stopped him."

"Won't you do it for me?" asked Mä'näbus smiling sweetly.

"Well, I'll try," said the newcomer and out he went.

When he got outside, the crowd asked him where he was going, and he told them.

"Oh, don't you do it," said the others. "Let someone else go in."

Another young man went in, only to be rebuffed in the same way. Mä'näbus insisted that he wanted to see Mud Turtle, and the other man went away discomfited.

At last a fourth tried his luck at courting, and when he too failed to meet with success, the crowd outside decided to call Mud Turtle, and the first man went to fetch him. When Turtle heard the message he did not believe it.

"You are just fooling me," he said. Then the second man went to him. "I do not believe you," was Turtle's reply. "You are deceiving me," he said to the third, but when the fourth one came he was convinced. "Oh well, maybe it's true," he thought, so he went to see.

"Oh Turtle," exclaimed Mä'näbus, when he came into the lodge. "I came here purposely to see you. I sent many times, but the men I told did not go."

"Why do you want to see me?" asked Turtle.

"Oh, I have often been told you are very powerful on account of your robe," said Mä'näbus. "I am so poor I just wanted to see you too because you are so handsome. If you will get your robe, you can sleep with me, and we will cover ourselves with it."

Turtle was completely deceived, and though he did not have the robe with him, she easily coaxed him to go get it. It was in his medicine bundle, and as he was taking it out, his grandmother asked him what he was doing. "Oh nothing, just getting my cloak out," replied Turtle.

When he returned, Mä'näbus inquired, "Have you got your bundle?"

"Yes indeed."

"All right, let's get the robe and cover ourselves all up with it," said Mä'näbus. So they put an extra blanket underneath and crawled in.

"What is your name?" asked Turtle.

"Wak´usikwé,"[2] replied Mä'näbus.

Then they covered themselves up so that no one could see what they were doing. Mä'näbus patted Turtle's head until finally he went to sleep and snored, "Hannhonh!"

Then Mä'näbus slipped out and, taking the cloak under his arm, ran out of the lodge. When he was safe outside, he let Marten go and hurried home. "You won't be anybody anymore, you Turtle," thought Mä'näbus as he ran off.

At this time, Mä'näbus had a great many dogs[3] no bigger than tiny puppies, and he kept them in a great wooden bowl. If at any time he desired to make them full size he would simply tell them to shake themselves, and they would grow at once. He gave Turtle's cloak to them, saying, "Whenever you are young, you will be spotted like that," and he covered them with it and went back to his house. Then he took off his woman's dress and flung it away.

Presently Turtle woke up and found himself alone. "Why I thought I was sleeping with a woman," he said. Then he began to call, "Wak´usikwé! Wak´usikwé!" running up and down and looking everywhere. "Where is she?" he asked. "I was sleeping with her." When he could not find her, he ran from house to house inquiring, but nobody else knew her name, for Mä'näbus had told it only to him.

Although Turtle searched everywhere, he was unable to find her. At last as he ran around he came to Mä'näbus' lodge.

"Come in and sit down," said Mä'näbus, and Turtle entered.

He was quiet for a long time, but finally he burst out, "You know everything all over the world. Have you ever heard of a woman called Wak´usikwé?"

"Why no, I have never heard of any such person," declared Mä'näbus, "but I have a little dog by that name. If you want to see her, she is covered up by that wooden pole over there."

"Well show me then," said Turtle.

"Oh! You go and look yourself. You are the one who has asked about her," said Mä'näbus.

So Turtle went and looked in, and there he saw two little dogs all spotted like his robe. He realized at once that he had been cheated. "Maaa! Mä'näbus," exclaimed Turtle. "Oh! have pity on me and give me back my robe."

"Why, I can't skin my dogs for you."

"Oh yes, indeed you can do that. You are so powerful," begged Turtle.

"Oh no," said Mä'näbus. "They are going to look that way as long as the world shall last."

Turtle kept on pleading.

"It is impossible," said Mä'näbus finally, "you did not have mercy on me at that feast. You called me an old woman. I can never forgive you. You know I was in mourning for my son. I am powerful. I can do anything I wish, and I have a place where you shall stay forever."

Then he seized Turtle by the neck and dragged him out and flung him into a muddy pond. "This is where you shall stay. You can look up once in a while," decreed Mä'näbus.

This story ends here.

Notes

1. Persons in mourning are not supposed to scratch with their hands.
2. Wak'usikwé means "Fox Woman" in Ojibway, but is a pun, for in Menomini it means "Egg Woman" or "Woman Full of Roe." In the Fox tale it is Ma'kosikawa or Doe Fawn. [Cf. "The Turtle Brings Ruin Upon Himself" which appears next in this volume. —JE]
3. Mä'näbus' dogs were really deer.

The Turtle Brings Ruin upon Himself (1907)

(Fox)

Recorder: William Jones

The Turtle was gambling with the manitous.[1] It happened that he had to go out to pass water. Whereupon Wīsa'kä took his place at the gambling. It so happened that they beat this (person) Wīsa'kä out of a good deal. They beat him out of all that the Turtle had previously won. It was about this time when back came the Turtle. And when he saw what they had done to him, then he gave his partner Wīsa'kä a thorough scolding. In this wise he lectured him: "There it is again! Verily, that is the way it has ever been since the time that Iyāpā'tä[2] was slain. Verily, that was the time when you began to eat the lice that dropped into your food without your helping it." Now that was the very thing he told his friend Wīsa'kä.

Whereupon it surely seemed that Wīsa'kä was angered. And so he began from that time to seek for a way to get back at the Turtle, his former friend. He felt indignant to be taunted with disrespect about his younger brother Iyāpā'tä. And so he went away and came to where he and the others lived.

And there he lay for a long while; for as much as four days was he in an ugly mood at what had been said to him. In this wise felt he in his heart: "Very much indeed was he a friend of mine in times past; but now it is not so. A time of reckoning is yet to come; according as I desire, so shall it happen to him, even if he has been such an intimate friend in the past. Ah, a thought occurs to me! Very deeply does he concern himself about women, so much so that he yearns after them. That is where I shall get back at him."

Accordingly went Wīsa'kä away on a journey. An elk he saw, and he killed it. He took from out of it the spleen and a vulva he made. So then he became a woman. In such guise he came to a lodge; but he did not enter there, instead passed he into the tiny little[3] lodge. Lo, to his surprise! it was a woman, MAnōnä by name, whose lodge he had entered.

This woman said: "Wait an instant, my little grandchild, there is nothing for you to sit on." So she made a pallet for the girl by laying down one skin of a small raccoon and another skin of a bear with the fat still on; one other small raccoon skin with the fat still on the girl was to use as a rest for the head. And when she had finished, she said to the girl: "All right, the vacant space is now ready for you to sit down on."

So she sat down, and it was soft where she sat.

Then MAnōnä cooked food for her in a small copper kettle; she cooked two grains of corn and a bean, and put with them the tail of a beaver. While the girl looked on, "Oh, dear me, I shall be quite hungry!" she felt in her heart.

"Never, my dear grandchild, has there been one among the manitous able to eat it all." Thus she spoke as she finished cooking the food (for the girl). Then she poured it out into a small bowl for (the girl), into a tiny little bowl. She fetched the food to the girl, and the girl ate. One by one she nibbled the little grains of corn, and for every one that she took out, there was always another to come in its place. But finally she was able to get away with them all, eating them up bit by bit.

"Here is your bowl," she said to MAnōnä. "Oh, no, my dear grandchild! You have eaten them all up!"

"Well, but you gave them to me to eat."

"My little grandchild, never has any one of the manitous, as many as they are, been able to eat them up. Verily, you must be a manitou, my dear grandchild."

"Oh, not at all," said the girl to her.

Thereupon MAnōnä cooked food for her in the regular way. While she cooked, she stole looks at the girl, and what a beautiful little woman she was! So she gave her food to eat once more, and heartily the girl ate; and when she was done eating, she had the feeling of having had enough [a satisfied fill inside].

Meanwhile, it was nearly time for the Turtle to show up. Had someone told him that there was a pretty little girl, and had he listened, it is certain that he would have been on his way there. After a while came the sound of his footstep. As he came inside, "Halloo, halloo!" he said to them there. Seating himself comfortably, he began to crumple the tobacco in his hands that he might smoke. The pouch for his pipe was the skin of a little baby.

"Gracious me!" said the woman; "but he surely is a mad kind of lover to come rushing into lodges of this sort,[4] passing in among them and hugging (the girls) so tight as to make them scream aloud." Thus spoke the old woman.

The Turtle had an easy place to sit, and he talked away at length. After a while he coughed and spat out a cowrie shell. The old woman made a grab for it. "Mercy, but you are filthy! Nasty are these things. At yonder place where I dwell is a lot of my spittle.[5] You would have much of it should you come there," thus said the Turtle.

He kept on talking until the young woman laughed. Into the night he talked on, and all the while the woman kept a-laughing. Finally he began to nudge her softly with the finger. Then no longer did the Turtle know what to talk about.

As for the old woman, MAnōnä, she made ready her pallet to lie down and went to sleep.

Presently the Turtle said to the woman: "You speak in too loud a tone. Speak softly." Thereupon he moved, sitting closer to the girl.

"I really am not able to speak in a low tone," said the girl.

There were present young men peeping in from the outside. "Ah, maybe the Turtle wants to get himself a bride!" they said (among themselves). And then they began to leave, going till they were all gone.

"I say, let us go out of doors," said the Turtle. "Then we shall talk as long as we want. It is nice what I have to tell about."

"Unless you go and fetch your sacred bundle, [otherwise] I will not believe what you say."

"Of course, I am telling only the truth. I will go and fetch the sacred bundle."

"When you have brought it here, then I will go outside."

So the Turtle took his departure and came to where he lived. He entered into the family dwelling and went to the place where his sacred bundle was. He reached up and took it down.

The brother saw what he was doing and said to him: "Pray, what are you doing? Are you going away to war?"

"Oh, be still, brother. Be content only with watching me. You are of no consequence, anyhow." Thus he spoke to his younger brother.

"It would not be strange if you were crazy!" he said to the Turtle.

Out of the lodge he went, carrying with him his sacred bundle. When he was come there at the place, "I now have the thing," he said to the girl.

Then she went out. Very beautiful indeed was she. To make sure of the thing, the woman took time to feel of the sacred bundle with her hand. "After all, you were telling the truth!" said she to him. "Now it is [quite] for you to decide as to where we shall go."

"Pray, what is your name, woman?"

"Why, Doe-Fawn is what I am called by my uncles and my aunts when they poke fun at me."

"And so that is your name! Truly, how very pretty your name is, woman. Oh, here is a place where we can keep on with our talk!"

"It is not necessary for you to feel that you must talk. You have already shown that you were telling the truth."

"Why, of course, that is so!"

So they made for themselves a place to lie down. Then after a little while the Turtle began to swell with an erection of the penis.

"Let us put something under our heads for a pillow," said the woman. So they lay with a pillow under their heads; the sacred bundle was the pillow.

Now was the time when the Turtle let his hand steal softly over her to find how big she was at the vulva. And then he went in unto her. It was hard work before he could make her possible; yet it was pleasant after he was done with her. She tickled him in the loins and would not let up until he went in unto her again. And when they were done he said to her: "I say, let us rest! Do, for a short while, little Doe-Fawn! Let us spin away at some yarns."

"I really am never in the habit of doing any such thing as that, so I have nothing to tell about. Now this thing which we are doing is surely more delightful. What good is to come from the spinning of tales, anyhow!"

"Ah, it is true that there is more pleasure in this kind of thing." And so he went in unto her again. By this time he was thoroughly fagged out. After a while, he was done with lying with her. And as they lay there together, he was bent on telling stories; but whenever he began a tale, she would close his mouth with her hand.

At last she said to him: "What do you want with the stories? (If you could not keep up this thing,) then you had no business to get me started in the first place."

"I say, let me alone for a little while. Do wait, then by and by it will be again."

"Pray, what is the matter with you? 'I wish to speak the truth' was what you certainly said a while ago. Now there is no sense whatever to be merely lying here all the time."

"Why, don't you take any delight at all in it? As for me, I am quite pleased with it." So he went in unto her again, this time he was a long while at it. She teased him more than ever, and he really had a hard time getting done. "Now, then, let us go to sleep, Doe-Fawn."

She tickled him in the loins and would not let him rest. But at last the Turtle fell asleep. She shook him hard, but he did not wake. Then the woman made ready and rose to her feet. She went in search of a log fallen to decay, and found one alive with ants. She brought it and placed it where he lay. The Turtle slept with it, and it crumbled when he took hold of it with the hand. Then, taking up the sacred bundle, she went away.

As for the Turtle, he was fast asleep. Something kept waking him, and he would always say: "Oh, be quiet, little Doe-Fawn!" After a while he grew wide awake. Wishing to pass his hand gently over the girl, he began to feel, and the touch of the body was strange. Thinking in his heart that he would look upon her, lo! it was a chunk of wood he was looking at. Behold! the woman was gone, and so was his sacred bundle.

He rose to his feet and whistled. "O Doe-Fawn!" he called. At last he shouted, sending his voice afar. Then finally he set out for home.

As he entered [within] he was asked by his brother, "Well, Mischievous, where is that thing you carried off a while ago? Have you gone and thrown it away?"

"Not at all, my little brother. I will surely bring it back. I am going on a hunt for it now, and I shall surely find it."

"Pray, what may have possessed you to have thrown it away?"

"Do stop talking to me, my little brother. I have not thrown it away, I assure you. A woman has hidden it from me. And I shall bring her also." So, putting tobacco into the pouch which held his pipe, he went out of the lodge.

He went away to where a manitou dwelt. He went inside and said, "I say, I have come to ask if you know of anybody who perchance goes by the name of Little Doe-Fawn?"

"I do not know her at all."

He went away again, and came to another dwelling, to a manitou dwelling. He went inside and said, "I say, I wish to ask you if there is anyone with such a name as Doe-Fawn? She took my sacred bundle and carried it away with her."

"Not at all do I know of anyone with such a name as that."

He went away again, and came to another dwelling, to a manitou dwelling. He went inside and said, "I say, I have come to ask you if there is anybody who would likely go by such a name as Doe-Fawn? She took my sacred bundle and carried it away with her."

"Not at all do I know of anybody with such a name as that. Yet that one over there might know about her. He is a great manitou. I would have you go there, and he will tell you. He probably knows about her. Why, he is the one who knows everything. He created us all."

In the meanwhile, the Turtle was becoming nothing but skin and bones, for it was a long time since he had eaten food. So he went away and came to where the great manitou lived. He entered [within] and said, "I say, I have come to ask you if there is anybody who would likely go by such a name as Doe-Fawn. If you know her, I should like to have you tell me. She took my sacred bundle and carried it away with her."

"No, not at all. I don't know of anybody who goes by that name. No, there is not anyone at all. I know all the manitous, but there is nobody of that name."

So he went away. Over there as he went traveling along, he happened to think of his friend Wisa'kä. "Now I have it. It is my friend! To him will I go. Surely will my friend not fail to know her. Yes, thither will I go, where he lives. Being a friend of mine, of course he will tell me." In such wise did he feel in his heart. So he went away to the place where (Wisa'kä) lived. When he was come, he passed inside.

"Welcome!" Wisa'ka said to him. "You must have been sick," the Turtle was told.

"Not at all, my friend. They have brought ruin upon me."

"Who?"

"A woman. She took my sacred bundle and went away with it. For that reason have I come, that I might ask you if you know of anybody who would go by such a name as Doe-Fawn?"

"Not at all do I know of anyone of that name. But I have some pet animals here, and I call them Little-Fawns. Yet I do not know how they could cause you harm. Go look at them. They are naughty little creatures."

"Alas it must have been my friend! He is the one who must have caused my ruin!" Thus he began to feel in his heart. So he went to look at the fawns and his friend came along as company.

"Well, here they are. Take a look at them."

So he looked at them. Lo! and there was his sacred bundle. It had been trampled and kicked quite into shreds. Only a little bit was left for him to see. Then he began to weep.

(Wīsa'kä) went up to him and took him by the tail. "You stung me with insult at the time when you taunted me about my younger brother."

"Woe is me! Don't my friend be too cruel with me!"

"Of course I will not be too cruel with you." Then he gave (him) a fling, throwing as if to hit a pond. And there was where (the Turtle) landed. In a little while he came to the surface of the water, there above the mossy scum which lay over the water.

"Now, that is the way it shall be with you. My uncles and my aunts will often use you for food. But some of them will not eat of you. They will loathe you because of your ugly look. So then I have nothing more to say to you."

That is the (end of the story).

Notes

1. This story is of the Turtle at the time when he was prominent among the manitous, and its motive is the fall of the Turtle from the state of being a great manitou. The cause that started him on his downward career was his incurring the anger of the culture hero who took on the form of a maiden and by

her wiles lured him on to his destruction; and the cause which completed his fate was the sacrilege he committed when he desecrated the sacred bundle. The story as recorded here has not a complete ending. It should tell of the gift made by the culture-hero to the Turtle—the gift of a certain kind of control over the soul in its attempt to get to the spirit-world in time of sickness.

2. Kīyāpā'tä[a] is another form of the name. Tcipiyāpōsu[a], lord of the spirit-world, is meant.
3. TcAgiwīgiyāpäheg[i], "into the tiny little lodge"; the reference is to the small lodge women occupy during the period of menstruation.
4. Wīgiyāpyän[i] mAnäciginig[i], "lodges of this sort." It is not lawful for a man to linger about the little lodge where a woman is menstruating, much less to enter it when she is there.
5. The form and color of the cowrie shell associate it with spittle, and this fact explains one reason why the shell is a convenient instrument for conjuring for effect to take place within the body.

Red-Hair's (Ici´oce) Hair (1918)

(Crow)

Recorder: Robert H. Lowie

A young man was going to marry a young girl.[1] She said, "If you'll bring me some of Red-hair's hair, you may marry me."

The young man went to another Indian and asked, "Who and where is Red-hair?"

"If I told you, should you go there?"

"Yes."

"Why should you go there?"

"I wanted to marry a young woman, and she said, 'If you bring me some of Red-hair's hair, I'll marry you.'"

The man pointed in a certain direction. "It is very far, you'll never get there."

"Yes, I'll get there." He took one hundred arrows and set out.

After a while, he came to a tipi, and in it sat a man. The one who told the youth about Red-hair advised him to kill a sheep and bring it to the man in the tipi in order to get his advice. So now the man asked, "Where are you going that you have brought this for me?"

"I am going to Red-hair."

"Why?"

"I wanted to marry a girl. She said, 'If you want to marry me, you must bring me some of Red-hair's hair!'"

"Those are strong people. I do not think you can do anything. You will get to a creek and see a white tipi there. Before you get to it, kill an elk and take it there."

When he left this adviser, he accordingly killed an elk and put it at the door of the white tipi. In it there was a man, who asked: "Where are you going? You have killed game for me. No one has ever done this before."

"I am going to see Red-hair."

"Why?"

"I wanted to marry a girl, and she will not marry me unless I fetch some of Red-hair's hair."

"They are strong people that you are going to. Now, when you leave this place, you will get to a river and find a white tipi there. Kill a female deer and bring it over. The owner of the tipi is a young woman. She will give you advice. When you come to the last tipi, I'll go there myself and help you, too."

The young man went to the next white tipi. He killed a female deer and brought it to the door. The girl came out, took the game, and bade him enter. "Where are you going to? You are all alone. Still you have come."

"I am going to Red-hair."

"Why do you want to go there?"

"I wanted to marry a girl. She said she would not marry me unless I brought some of Red-hair's hair."

"He is a strong man. A little way from here, there is a little creek. There is a white tipi there standing all alone. Kill a female antelope and bring it to the door. The one in the tipi will give you advice, and I'll go there, too, and help you."

The young man went on, killed an antelope, and put it at the door. A woman came out and found it.

"Where are you going? No one has ever done this before."

"I saw your tipi and thought I'd kill some game for you."

"Where are you going?"

"I am going to Red-hair."

"Why?"

"I wanted to marry a girl, and she won't marry me unless I fetch some of Red-hair's hair."

"You are going to a powerful one. Stop and I'll give you advice."

Now the girl he had seen before and the two men also came to the tipi, and all four debated. "What can we do, so he'll be able to get the hair?" Each one gave his opinion.

One of the men said: "All of us earth people are lecherous. We'll have to make use of this in order to get it."

They agreed upon this.

One of the young women was a whitetail deer, the other an ant. The men asked these two to help the young man. So one of them took the tops of two anthills and made breasts out of them for the man's body, and the other gave him her vulva. Then they called the wolverine and asked him to change the young man into a woman. When he had done so, one of the men was told to embrace the transformed young man. He said that he was just like a woman now.

Now they advised him. "It is not good for you to get too close. For watchers he has the coyote and the crane. When anything comes close, the crane will hoot and the coyote will howl. This is the signal. Then they have dogs and a big wolf and one snake watcher. These are dangerous. For a short time after noon, the crane and the coyote fall asleep. When you get to a ridge, change yourself into a little ant and travel as fast as possible. The dogs are not so particular and when you have passed them change back again. You will get to a tipi and chief Red-hair will see you all alone. He will fall in love with you, and you must tell him that you want to marry Red-hair."

He started out. He got to the ridge and turned into an ant. He went as fast as possible. Both the crane and the coyote were asleep. Dogs were watching, but the ant passed between them. The crane woke up, but it was too late.

Red-hair saw the woman. "I wonder how this woman came here in spite of all the watchers." He asked her, "Why have you come?"

"I came to marry the chief Red-hair."

"You want to marry me; you may sit here."

She sat beside him. The last young woman advised the young man to get to her tipi as soon as possible after getting his hair.

Red-hair's brothers came back from the chase. "How is this?" they asked.

"She came to marry me, and I have married her." So they cooked food for her.

Some time after this, they returned from hunting and gave food to the couple, saying to the chief, "Take this, Wife-man's-arm."

They went on another hunt, came back with food, cooked it, and gave it to the woman, saying, "Sister-in-law-man's-arm" (búakbatsɛ'-a´re). When the young man was transformed, they had forgotten to change his arms, which remained scarred.[2]

The woman said to her husband: "Your brothers say my arms are a man's. They are insulting me. I have had children, and when I mourned for them, I got these scars."

So Red-hair told his brothers not to insult his wife and that she had had to mourn for relatives.

One of the brothers said: "Is your wife a woman? Do you have marital relations with her?"

"Many times."

"That may be, but she has the breath of a man.[3] To prove it, let her go out of the tipi door. She'll have the step of a man."

Her husband got angry. "She's a woman. Don't you see her breasts? I have had marital relations with her all the time."

"We'll find out sooner or later whether she is a man."

The transformed young man stayed there with Red-hair for a long time. One day the woman was lousing him,[4] and his face was on her lap. She touched the tender part at the back of his head. He was asleep. She felt for the tender part, took a knife, and stabbed him. He made no outcry, but simply gave one kick, and died. She got his hair as best she could. She went out. The dogs paid no attention to her. The crane, looking through the smoke hole, saw that his master was bald-headed, and began to hoot. The coyote howled. The young man had deer power, hence was a good runner, and began to run now. Red-hair's brothers were out butchering, but they heard the crane and the coyote. They said, "Just as we said, that fellow who was married to him must be at the bottom of this." They went home and saw their brother bald-headed. They followed the fugitive's tracks.

He had already got to the site of the girl's tipi, but there was no tipi there, only a little anthill. Under it was a large hole. He went through the hole and got to the site of the second tipi, where there was a vine. The pursuers saw the ants and thought they were too harmless to trick them.

"Have you seen anyone?"

"Yes, we saw a whitetailed deer."

They got to the whitetailed deer woman. "Have you seen anything pass here?"

"Yes, a whitetailed deer."

They got to the first man, and he said, "There is an eagle that flew past here. He seemed to be in great haste."

They got to the fourth adviser. He said, "I saw a white hawk flying as fast as possible; he looked as though he were running away."

"How long ago was this?"

"A rather long time ago. He was going so fast I don't think you can catch up."

Then the brothers said, "We are helpless." They turned back.

A swallow was sent to watch them go. It followed them to their place and reported that they had got home. The young man came out of the last tipi. He had the hair of Red-hair. He went home to his own people. He gave the hair to the girl. "Here is what you wished for." He married her.

Notes

1. Cf. Wissler and Duvall, 129, 132 footnote.
2. Cf. Dorsey and Kroeber, 131 for a striking parallel.
3. It's possible that *breath* is a typo and, given the context, that *breadth* is likely the correct word. —JE
4. This detail is likewise found in the same Arapaho tale.

Pregnant Men

The Chief's Son Who Received the Animal Power (1906)

(Pawnee)

Narrator: White-Sun

Recorder: George A. Dorsey

A long time ago, the people had their village upon the Republican River. In the village was a fine-looking young man who was a son of the chief. The young man was very kind and was good to everybody. There was a man who became very fond of the chief's son, and one day, he came to him and said, "I would like to talk with you and take you to a faraway country." The boy, suspecting nothing, promised to go with the man, and so they prepared for their journey and started.

They traveled for many days until at last they came to a place known as Pahuk. They went to a steep bank and sat down. The man began to tell the boy that there had been stories told about this wonderful place and that he had brought him there because he wanted to tie a rope around his waist and let him down over the steep bank to pick up some eagle and woodpecker's feathers which were upon the bank.

The man put a lariat around the boy's waist and let him down the steep bank. When the boy reached the bank, he began to pick up the feathers. He then looked up to tell the man to pull him up, but the man was not there, and there were no signs of him. The boy cried for help, for he was in trouble. On the journey he had become pregnant, and gradually grew larger all the time until, when he was upon the bank, he knew that he was about to give birth. Then he cried, and yelled, and called to the man to pull him up, but the man had run away and left the boy hanging on the side of the steep bank so that he would die. The boy cried until he was exhausted, and then he went to sleep.

The animals came out from under the bank and found the boy. When they saw him they said, "Let us take pity on him," and they carried him into their lodge.

When the boy awoke, he saw all kinds of animals and birds, and he was surprised. The Buffalo was the first to speak. He said, "Let us help this poor boy. We know what the trouble is. He has been bewitched."

All the animals agreed, and the Elk was the first to stand up and run towards the boy. The Elk jumped over the boy, and when he jumped over the boy, the other animals saw blood in the Elk's mouth. Then the Buffalo ran and jumped over the boy, and there was blood in his mouth.

Each animal took his turn, and then they all ran busily about in the lodge. The dust rose towards the sky, so that the boy could not be seen.

The Bear came to where the boy was and stopped. The Bear screamed, then took one of his claws and cut the boy open. He took out the bones of the child, threw them away, and healed the wound. The boy was then told to sit up.

Then the Snake came and said, "My son, I am bad. I kill people. I can kill you by spitting upon you. I give you this bone. Strike the enemy with this bone that I have given you and it will kill them."

The Buffalo came and said, "I will teach you something. Take this whistle." Upon the center of the whistle was painted a buffalo skull. "When you get into trouble, whistle, and I will be with you. I will make you brave so that you shall get out of trouble."

Then the Bear came and said, "My son, I can kill people. Look at me." The Bear at this time was on his four feet, and when he arose, there was a great dust. When the dust passed by, the Bear blew his breath and the dust came from his mouth. He told the boy to take a little dust and put it into the sack. It was to be used as a paint to put upon the sick people and upon the wounded.

Then a Buffalo cow came and said, "I can kill people." She made a great dust about the boy.

Each animal taught the boy some mystery; then they told him that he must return to his people. Before they let him go, they told him that they must teach him some sleight-of-hand performances. The Eagles taught the boy how to fly. The Ducks taught him how to swim and dive. The animals then said that the boy was hungry and that they wanted to feed him. They sent the Crow into the west, and the Beaver into the north, and the Otter into the east, and the Hawk into the south to bring food for the boy.

While these animals were away to get something for the boy to eat, one of the animals spoke to the boy and said, "We know what the man did to you. He tried to poison you. He tried to make you like a woman. We have taught you great mysteries. If you desire, you can bewitch him."

After the animals came back with something to eat, and the boy had eaten, the leading animal of the lodge, who was a Beaver, said, "My boy, it is time to go home. The animals will show you the way. The Owl, Buffalo, and two Crows will be the ones to lead you to your home. They will stop outside the village. Enter the village, but do not let the people know that you are there. The next day after you arrive, take the man who tried to poison you to the river and swim with him. Our animals will go up the stream and they will bewitch him."

When the Beaver finished speaking, the Crow came near to the boy and touched him, and the boy found himself outside of the lodge of the animals. Then he was told to try to fly, and he arose in the air and flew like a crow.

They left the boy just outside of his village. In the night, the boy went into the village to the lodge of his father and spoke to him. The father did not believe that his son, whom he had mourned for as dead, could have returned. He made his wife make a fire, and then he saw that it was his son, and he was glad. The next day, the people heard that the boy had returned. They came from all directions to see the boy and to give him presents. Then the boy sent for the man who had injured him, and when the man came, the boy picked up a bucket and said, "Come with me down to the creek." When the boy was dipping water, the other man touched the water. As soon as he touched the water he was dragged under. The man disappeared and was never seen again. When the boy came up, he told the people that the man was a witch, but for them not to be afraid, as he had disposed of him and that he would never return to trouble them.[1]

Note

1. The story teaches that it is impossible to deceive the animals. Especially does it illustrate the dire consequences befalling one who betrays a friend.

Nänabushu Pretends to Be a Woman (1917)

(Ojibwa)

Narrator: Wâsāgunackạng

Recorder: William Jones

And then away he started upon his journey, travelling afoot. And so he came within the sound of some women who were gathering firewood; now he secretly overheard them saying: "I wonder how we can bring it to pass so that we can marry that man!" they said.

"Now, a trick I am going to play on them, whoever they are," thought Nänabushu. He knew that the mother (of the man) would cry. And so he got into gay attire after he had taken on the form of a woman. There was a caribou spleen which he turned into a woman's thing. After he had taken on the form (of a woman), (and) after he had gone over to where the women were, this he then said to them when he came upon them: "Where is the man who is said to be a hater of women?"

Whereupon he was told: "Here in the centre of the town he is," he was told. "He is hopelessly impossible. It is uncertain what his feeling would be (concerning you)."

"Then pray, do you go and give him a message," he said to them. "I have been sent hither by my parents," he said to the women.

And so truly, when back one (of them) went, then was the old woman who was mother (to the man) given the message.

Then said the woman who had conveyed the message: "A stranger is here. And this she said, 'I have been sent hither by my parents,' she said. And so when I was set upon my way hitherward, 'Go give the news,' I was told. I was loath (to go). 'Let my friends come hither,' (said the woman)."[1]

Thereupon said the old woman[2]: "Why do you not go look for her?"[3] she said to her daughters.

And so truly came the women seeking for her, whereupon back home the women went, taking her[4] with them. And then a place was made for her there where the man [5] was seated. Therefore, she[6] now had a husband.[7] By and by, she wished her sisters-in-law to go with her to gather firewood.[8] So in a little while after the sound of her chopping was heard, already (was there) much firewood.

"Who is she that is such a remarkable worker?" they said to their mother, they said to her, telling her about it. "Truly a good worker is our sister-in-law."[9]

Now, thoroughly pleased was the old woman, as was also the old man, that such a good worker was their daughter-in-law.[10]

And then she (Nänabushu) addressed the Marten, saying: "I wish you would help me in this that I am undertaking," she said to it. And so that was the creature she had for child, and this she said to it: "Come, now, all the while do you cry," she said to it. And that truly was what (the Marten) did. When she had it strapped to the cradle-board, her arrangement was such that she had it bound up as far as over the eyes; with it bound to the cradle-board, she played the nurse carrying it about on her back.

And so all the while did (the Marten) weep.

"Now, this do you say," she said to it. "'Some tenderloin do I wish to eat,' do you say, so that you may cry," she said to it.

And that truly was what the infant cried. "Some tenderloin do I want to eat!" it cried.

Presently they understood what it wanted.

Now, then out went her father-in-law to cry aloud, for he was chief; for of necessity were the people bound to do whatever the old man should say. "Now, O ye people! Thus says my grandchild, 'Some tenderloin do I want to eat,'" he said. And so truly was Nänabushu given some tenderloin. It hushed when it was given something good to eat.

And so while she (Nänabushu) continued living (as a wife) with the man, she then became aware that the spleen was decaying. And so one morning, while her father-in-law and mother-in-law were seated, she then began to realize that she was becoming rotten between the loins.

"Phew!" said her father-in-law. "What is that which smells so?" said her father-in-law.

Truly was she worried about it. When she rose to her feet, in vain she tried to keep it from falling. When she dropped it in front of where her father-in-law was seated, then away she started running.

"Truly a real woman they thought!" said Nänabushu.

Notes

1. The woman impersonated by Nänabushu.
2. A woman to whom the message had been given.
3. The woman impersonated by Nänabushu.
4. The woman impersonated by Nänabushu.
5. The woman-hater.
6. The woman impersonated by Nänabushu.
7. The formality of leading a daughter to that part of a lodge where a man seats himself, and having her seat herself by him, is the public announcement that she is his wife.
8. One of the things a bride does is to go for firewood or for water, a convention by which she enters her new station.
9. A pleasing compliment which a wife enjoys is to hear it said of her that she is a good worker.
10. Pleased because their maintenance is assured. A son is seldom encouraged to marry a woman simply because she is handsome or that she is of a pleasing disposition; but if she can work, if she can turn her hands to something useful, then she is the one for him to get. Behind all this is the desire of the old folks to be cared for in their old age.

Tasinta-Yukikipu (1893)

(Dakota)

Recorder: Stephen Return Riggs

Behold, thus it was: There were four young men, and one was who was called Hakaykayna. These lived together. And so it was that, when they went hunting, they made the youngest one the keeper of the house and said to him, "My youngest brother, don't go anywhere. Stay at home." Saying this, they went to hunt, and he watched the house. Now the house they lived in was a very long one, but all around the inside, the packs were piled up on each other, and also there were scaffolds on the outside, for every day they brought home all kinds of wild animals, and so they had a great abundance of meat.

And so, on a time, they went out to hunt, and Hakaykayna watched the house, but when he was lonesome, he went out to cut arrow sticks, and when something pierced his foot [so] that it was very sore, he started home. When he reached the house, he opened the sore place, and, lo! he took out a girl baby.

And on account of this, Hakaykayna, sad of heart, wrapped a blanket around it, and laid it back, and so was silent. "Oh that it might grow up!" he thought, and so was sad of heart until all his brothers came home from the hunt. He had always been glad when they came home, but it was not so now.

They judged something had made him sad, and so they said to him, "My brother, what makes you sad of heart? If anyone has done anything to you, tell us."

But he said, "No one has done anything to me, but I have seen what makes me heartsore and silent."

And they said, "What is it?"

And he said, "Brothers, when you went away, I was lonesome and went out to cut arrow sticks, and something stabbed my foot, and it was very sore, so that I came home. When I reached home and took it out, it was a baby that I pulled out, and it was a girl baby, perhaps. 'Oh, that it might grow up!' I thought, and on that account I am heartsore."

And his brothers said, "Where is it?"

So he took it up and showed it to them, and they passed it from one to another, and said, "Oh, that it might grow up!"

Then Hakaykayna said, "My brothers, come, let us whirl it around the house." So they took it up and threw it out of the roof hole, and it whirled around and fell down. But now it was a creeping baby and came in crying. Again they took it up and whirled it as before, and then she came in walking, a little girl. But again they took her up and threw her, and she came in a girl bringing sticks of wood, which she placed on the fire. But again they took her up and threw her as before. This was the fourth time they whirled her, and then she came with a back-load of wood. She untied the strap, and came in the house, and sat down.

Then they asked, "What relation shall she be to us?"

And one said, "My youngest brother found her. Let him take her for his wife."

But Hakaykayna said, "No, that shall not be so."

And they said, "What then shall be her relation to us?" And [they] mentioned several terms of relationship.

But Hakaykayna did not consent.

"What then," they said, "shall we have her for? What do you want?"

And he said, "This one came after us. Let us have her for younger sister."

They all said, "That is the proper thing." So they made her a bed and placed her in the back part of the house.

Now she was very skillful in needle and quill work. She embroidered quivers, moccasins, knife sheaths, and carrying-straps for them, so that they greatly rejoiced.

When they were to go out hunting, they said, "Now, my brother, watch over sister well."

But when he grew tired, he said, "Now sister, do you watch. I will go and cut a green arrow stick." He went and soon came back, but his sister was not there. He thought she had gone for a little while, and so waited for her to come home. But when she came not for a long while, he went to hunt her.

Not finding her, he came in and waited until his brothers came home and said to him, "My brother, where is sister?"

When he told them about it, they said, "Alas, alas! where has our sister gone?" And they waited, and it became dark, and Hakaykayna cried, and the brothers all cried with him.

Then the oldest one said, "My brothers, stop crying. Soon it will be morning; this island earth is small; we will then see what has made us cry." So now, when the morning came, they started out to each of the four winds, and they went all over the earth. And when they found her not, they were very sad and cut off their hair as they wept.

When they had ceased to hunt for her, Hakaykayna every day went abroad and walked around crying. One day, after crying around, he fell asleep, and lo! on waking up, he heard someone crying somewhere. But not hearing it distinctly, he went to a high hill and stood on it. Then, lo! somewhere he heard a woman wail out in her crying, "Brothers, who are called Tasintayookeekeepee, brothers, who once cared for me tenderly, for four seasons, I have had a hard time."

This he heard and said, "Well! that seems to be sister somewhere," and so he started home crying. When he arrived his brothers cried too, but he said, "My brothers, cease and boil the kettle; we will drink some soup." So they cooked and ate. Then Hakaykayna said, "My brothers, who are they who are called Tasintayookeekeepee?"

The eldest one answered, "Of all people we only are all males, and hence are so called. But why do you ask that?"

And he said, "I heard a woman wail out that as she cried."

"Alas, alas! that is probably our sister," they said, and they stood in the fire.

But Hakaykayna said, "Brothers, cease; if indeed this is our sister, she is alive, and we shall perhaps see her again," and he cried.

Now when the morning came, they went and stood with him where he had heard the voice. He said, "Yes, this is where I heard it."

Then they heard her again saying, "My brothers who are called Tasintayookeekeepee, brothers who cared for me tenderly, for four seasons, I have had a hard time."

They heard this cry and said, "Yes, this is our sister," and they all cried.

But Hakaykayna said, "Stop, we shall indeed see our sister in a part of a day, and I will see her first." So saying, he changed himself into a chickadee, and went in, and saw his sister lying with her limbs fastened and her face covered with sores. He alighted by her, but she did not think it was one of her brothers.

And so she said, "Chickadee, if I could only see my brothers, I would embroider your breast around."

And the chickadee said, "My sister, it is I."

She said, "Brother, let us go home."

But he said, "Presently, my sister. We have now found you. Tell all about it."

And she said, "Brother, the otters brought me home. They dug from within the earth, and made a hole up to where I was, and dragged me in. Then they closed up the hole in the earth so that you could not come find me."

When she had said this, he said, "Yes, I will go for my brothers." When he came home to his brothers, he said, "It is our sister." And they went with him. And they came to a house that was stretched out very long, outside of which their sister was placed with her forelimbs fastened.

Then she said, "My brothers, I have been now four seasons in this suffering state, but I am still alive, as you see me. That is owing to one thing, of which I will tell you. There are five kinds of otters here; one is red, one is blue, one is yellow, one is white, and one is black. It is because of the last one that I am alive, brothers. When they boiled fish and threw out the bones they emptied the bones and the hot soup upon me, so that I am burned by the heat, and the bones pierced me so that my face is all sore. That is the reason of my being so. But when the black otter came to empty out the bones, he would put into my mouth some of the meat and of the soup also. On account of that, you see me alive. Therefore, my desire is that the black otter may live.

"When the evening comes, then they return from their hunts. When the red one comes, he makes red lightning shimmer through the house; when the blue one comes, he lights up the house with blue lightning; when the yellow one comes, he makes yellow lightning shoot through the house; when the white one comes, he makes white lightning shine through the house."

Now, when her brothers had made themselves war clubs, they took their stations at each side of the door of the long house. Now it came to pass when the red lightning gleamed through the house and the red otter put his head in at the door and said, "My house smells of something," then they killed him and drew him inside the house. Then, again, the blue lightning gleamed through the house, and as he said, "My house smells of something," he put in his head, but they killed him and drew him into the house. The yellow lightning gleamed through the house, and the yellow otter, saying, "My house smells of something," pushed in his head, but they killed him and pulled him into the house. By and by, a white lightning gleamed through the house, and a white otter pushed in his head, but they killed him also and drew him into the house.

Then the black otter came home, and the sister said, "That is the one that did it." So they took him alive. Then they cut all the cords that bound their sister and washed the sores on her face, after which they took her and the otter to their home. Now when they had come home, they watched over their sister better, and they took good care of the otter that they saved alive. But he was always sad of heart, and as he sung to himself, he said, "Brothers Haypan! Brothers Haypan! I said we ought to use a different ladle; you did not listen to me, and I, the bad-furred one, alone am saved. Brothers Haypan! Brothers Haypan!"

And they said this to him, "You did well to us, and therefore, we want to treat you well, but if you are going to be always sad of heart, you shall do what pleases you; if you want to go where you please, so you shall do."

And he said, "Yes, I want to be free to go where I please."

And they said to him, "Go, you shall be called the Western Child Otter." And they let him go.

Therefore, they say it is that now there are only black otters.

Love Between Women

Lesbian Love (1909)

(Assiniboine)

Recorder: Robert H. Lowie

A man was living with his wife and sister. The woman wished to have intercourse with the girl. While her husband was hunting, she eloped with her sister-in-law. The man did not know where they could have gone. He looked for them in the camp, and finally concluded that they had been killed. He grieved very much over their death.

In midwinter, he once went out hunting. Remembering the two women, he began to cry. He thought they must have perished in the cold. He ascended a hill. There he heard a noise. He had no gun or knife; nevertheless, he walked towards the sound. His wife and sister being dead, he also wished to die. Towards sunset he reached the place where he had heard the noise and caught sight of a human head. He recognized his sister and immediately guessed that his wife was also there.

Stepping nearer, he saw smoke rising from among the bushes and heard a child crying by the fireplace. He could hear the women talking. His wife was playing with the infant. He knew that she must have married his sister. He saw his sister nursing the child.

Approaching, he asked, "Which of you has seduced the other?"

His sister answered, "Your wife persuaded me to elope with her."

The infant was continually crying. It looked like a football; it had no bones in its body because a woman had begotten it. The man killed the child, then he bade the women go home. When they were near the camp, he told his sister to walk ahead. Then he killed his wicked wife with his knife. His sister ran to camp and told a man she met that her brother was slaying his wife, begging him to save her. But before the stranger arrived, the husband had killed his wife and severed her limbs from the body. He did not kill his sister. Though the slain woman had many relatives, none cared to avenge her death.[1]

Note

1. Cf. Jones, p. 151 (Fox)

Two Maidens Who Played the Harlot with Each Other (1907)

(Fox)

Recorder: William Jones

It is said that once a time long ago there were two young women who were friends together. It is told that there were also two youths who tried to woo the two maidens, but they were not able even so much as to talk with one another. After a while the youths began to suspect something wrong with them. It is reported that this took place in the summer.

So it is said that once during the summer the two maidens started away to peel off bark. The youths followed after, staying just far enough behind to keep within sight of them. (The girls) went a long way off, and over there is where they stripped off bark. While (the girls) were peeling the bark, (the youths) all that time kept themselves hidden from them.

After a while (thc youths) no longer heard the sound of (the maidens) at work. Whereupon they began to creep up to where they were. When they drew nigh, behold, the maidens were then in the act of taking off their clothes! The first to disrobe flung herself down on the ground and lay there. "Pray, what are these (girls) going to do?" was the feeling in the hearts of (the youths). And to their amazement the girls began to lie with each other!

Thereupon one of the youths whistled, and both together ran up to where (the girls) were. One that was lying on top instantly fell over backwards. Her clitoris was standing out and had a queer shape, it was like a turtle's penis.

Thereupon (the maidens) began to plead with (the youths): "Oh, don't tell on us!" they said to them. "Truly, it is not of our own free desire that we have done this thing. We have done it under the influence of some unknown being."

It is said that afterwards one of the maidens became big with child. In the course of time, strange to relate, she gave birth; and the child was like a soft-shell turtle![1]

Note

1. This is an account of how two young women had sexual intercourse with each other and how, as a result of the unnatural union, one gave birth to an unnatural offspring.

VIOLENCE AND THE TWO-SPIRITS

The Coyote Called "Another One" (1942)

(Western Mono)

Recorder: Edward Winslow Gifford

Yellow jacket had three sons, all coyotes. The three went down to spear salmon at Italian Bar on the San Joaquin river. Another coyote came by; he was a male also. He went to Yellow jacket's three sons and asked them their names. They replied that their name was Coyote. Thereupon the stranger coyote said, "That is not my name. Your names are different from mine. Go to Jackrabbit and ask him my name. He knows it."

The stranger coyote, accompanied by one of the three coyote brothers, proceeded to Jackrabbit's habitation. As they went along, the stranger coyote fell behind, so that his companion approached Jackrabbit first. Jackrabbit greeted him, saying, "Hello, Coyote."

Then when the stranger coyote came in sight, Jackrabbit exclaimed, "Oh! Here is another one."

Then the stranger coyote said to the other coyote, "I told you that Coyote was not my name. My name is Another One."

The two returned to where the others were still spearing salmon. All the while the stranger coyote was wishing that he might be a woman, for he wanted to cohabit with one of the brothers. He hit upon an idea and decided to go home. "I am going home," he said to the three brothers. Upon arriving at home, he hung himself by his hind legs. That changed him into a woman.

Next morning he repaired again to the place where the three brothers were spearing salmon. He sat nearby for a long while, then he arose and proceeded towards the three. One of them said, "Another One is coming."

Another brother said, "No. It is a woman coming."

The third disagreed and said, "It is Another One."

They joked with one another as to who should marry the woman, if it really were one. Finally the youngest said, "I am going to marry her, and I am going to take her home. Mother will help care for her."

The other two brothers said, "We will stay here. You take her home immediately."

"Let us go home," the youngest brother said to the stranger coyote who now appeared as a woman. On the way home they tried to cohabit. The youngest brother then discovered that his would-be bride was a male. He did not let the impostor know that he was aware of this fact, but he made an excuse to return to his brothers, saying that he had forgotten something.

While returning to the fishing place, he met a number of cowboys who were seeking Another One, because he had stolen something from them. With them he returned to his two brothers. Then it was that it became known that they were seeking "Another One," although the cowboys did not know him by that name.

Then the youngest brother returned with the cowboys, to show them where he had left Another One. They found him fast asleep. They put a rope around his neck, skinned him alive, and turned him loose. He came to the three brothers, who laughed at him. They nearly laughed themselves to death.

Another One cried at every twig that touched him, for being nothing but raw flesh, he was bleeding all over.

Falcon Captures the Cannibal Berdache (1940)

(Yokut)

Narrator: Sam Osborn

Recorders: A. H. Gayton and Stanley S. Newman

Berdache was a cannibal. He went around tying men up and cooking them. His talismans of supernatural power were a winnowing tray and a pestle. He threw them at his victims and killed them.

Falcon and his younger brother, Chicken Hawk, were living at Limikitri (falcon home). This was before the world was made.[1] The two hawks were traveling far west in the valley and wanted to get home. Berdache saw them; he threw his tray at Hawk and killed him. He cut off one of his legs and stuck it in his belt. Falcon was going toward home as fast as he could, but he was still about twenty miles away. Berdache said, "I don't care where you go; I'll kill you." He kept throwing his tray and pestle at Falcon, but they just grazed him and took off a few feathers.

Falcon was nearing home. He said, "My rock home, you open up so I can go through, then close up on this man behind me." It happened just that way. Berdache got caught between the rocks.[2]

Berdache called out, "My friend, let me go. I'll be your friend."

"Give me all my friends' feet, and I'll let you go."

"How much money will you take to let me go?" said Berdache.

"No, I don't care for money. I want my friends. Then I'll let you go, and we'll all be friends together."

Berdache conceded to this. Falcon went close so Berdache could hand the bones up to him. Berdache kept telling Falcon to come a little closer, hoping that he could catch him unaware. But Falcon came no closer; he made Berdache stretch as far as he could. Falcon knew how many legs there should be; Berdache was keeping one back. This was Hawk.

"I haven't got him," said Berdache.

"I can't let you go unless you give me my little brother."

Berdache waited a long time. Finally he gave up the last foot.

Falcon had a fox-skin quiver. This was his talisman. He did not want to let Berdache go until he had brought his friends to life. He took a deer arrow out of the quiver and holding a foot in his left hand struck it sharply with the arrow. It came to life and its owner stood before him. He did this to everyone. Some of them said, "I went to sleep."

"No," Falcon answered, "I'll explain to you very soon."

Then they all were returned to life and stood around. Finally Falcon called Road runner, Dove, and Crow to come to the rock and look at Berdache. He told them what had happened and warned them not to go too close. They asked Falcon, the chief, what he was going to do. He told the trio to go fetch wood, to pile it up under this man, and burn him up. Road runner ran all around making a pile of wood as high as he could reach with his feet. Then Dove made some fire with a buckeye hand drill. Berdache began to shout, asking to be free, offering all kinds of money and bribes. Falcon refused and burned him up until the ashes were completely cold.

Notes

1. Before the coming of human beings.
2. The rock where this occurred is to be seen but I [Sam Osborn—JE] don't know the exact location. The smoke stains show through a big crack in the rocks. Every kind of bird lives there. In little cracks in the rocks are rows of flowers that Hummingbird has stuck there. Falcon spoke in the Wobonuch language, Berdache in Tachi.

The Sioux Woman Who Acted as a Man (1903)

(Sioux)

Recorder: Alfred L. Kroeber

Among the Sioux, there was a woman whose parents were good and kept her dressed finely, but she wanted to dress as a man. Her father was displeased at her immodesty.

A war party started against the Pawnees, and she went along, wearing men's clothing. She struck many enemies, was unwounded, and achieved much honor. After the return of the party, the Sun-dance was made.

The woman said: "I know you do not like my conduct. You are ashamed of me. I cannot be killed by the enemy in war, but anyone in the tribe can kill me. Let some man kill me."

Then her father dressed her as a man.

The woman mounted a good horse, stood in front of her father's tent, closed her eyes, and said: "I am ready."

Then the man who had been selected shot her.

The Hehe'ya Trick Hüi'ki (1929)

(Hopi)

Recorder: Alexander M. Stephen

At Kishyu'ba dwelt the Hü'iki kachina.[1] The Hehe'ya are industrious, but they are *siwahova*.[2] The Hü'iki were one day working in their fields and the Hehe'ya came to help them. About noon, the Hü'iki, being hungry, said to the Hehe'ya, "Go you to the village and tell our wives to give you some food and bring some out to us."

And as they were starting on this errand, the Hü'iki said, "By what name are you people known? How shall we call you?"

The Hehe'ya said, "We are called *i'ich chova* (hasten to copulate)."

When they reached the village, they found the women preparing wafer bread and other food, and having delivered their message, the women set food before them and made bundles of food for them to take out to the fields.

After the Hehe'ya had eaten, they said to the women, "Your husbands also said that you should copulate with us."

But the women said, "Surely you are liars; go away; take the food out to the fields and do not speak so foolish."

But the Hehe'ya had loitered so long that the men in the fields were growing impatient and began to call them to hasten their return.

The cunning Hehe'ya expected this, so they said to the women, "Surely we are speaking the truth, but if you do not believe us, listen to your husbands."

So the women listened, and sure enough, they heard the men calling from the fields, "*I'ich chova!*" and being thus convinced, they yielded themselves to the Hehe'ya, who gave no more thought to carrying the food for the field workers.

After a while, the Hü'iki came in to the village, and discovering the trick that had been put upon them, they lashed the Hehe'ya with yucca and drove them away.[3]

Notes

1. *Hüi'kita,* to growl. They are not a dog kachina; they are men, but they are always angry and growling.
2. A man that no woman will marry, *ho'vo,* hermaphrodite; *siw'a,* sister?; *sihü,* flower?
3. For this European tale, see *F.F. Communications,* no. 74, 1563.

Didactic Myths

The Hopi Ghost Kills and Gambles (1928)

(Tewa)

Narrator: "I" of San Juan

Recorder: Elsie Clews Parsons

This story belongs to the Hopi.[1] Those Kosso (Hopi) have lots of *pinang*. There was fighting where they lived in their houses. They lived at Tsi' kwaiye. Then they beat those who came to fight them and they ran after them. A distance from here[2] to San Juan they went fighting, and one Hopi man was killed. They left him there. They did not tell him after four days to go away.[3] Because he had no heart, he was a kind of wind, he stood up then and he walked around all the world and he found no friends. So he came back to his house. They did not see him, because he was a kind of wind.

He went into a hill, in a big hole there at the end of the hill he lived. So at night he went out from where he lived. He went into the town and into every house. And he had a broom. So while they were sleeping with their wives, he took his (broom) straw and put it into their nostrils and played with them. They did not see him, he was a kind of wind. Those he played with did not wake up alive. The people did not know why they were all dying.

They said, "Wonder why this is going on? All the good girls and good boys are dying."

So the old ones called all the men and women into one kiva. All went, and that Summer chief said, "Now we have called all you children. I do not know why we are losing you all, boys and girls. They are not sick, and yet they die. That is what I am thinking about," said the Summer chief. "We must find out why it is so. We must look around this place where we live."

So they said, "Yes, that is what is passing here." They talked about it. They got a big boy (*enu*).[4]

"Our son," said the old man, "you ought to think like a woman and a man. Now we have you. Look around this place where we live. If we think about good things, maybe we shall find out who is doing this."

So he said, "Of course I will be a woman and a man. Because in this place we do not have good times."

So they made him stay in that place. And he ate nothing but medicine (*wo'*), and the Summer chiefs and Winter chiefs and the old men and Outside chiefs were taking care of him.

In four days he got thin from not eating anything. In five days in the night they went into the kiva. So they all stayed in the kiva. They began to sing. They took their eagle feathers and stood the youth up (with the ends of the feathers) and they sat him down on the road.[5]

They said, "Think like a woman and a man and like our father." So they smoked and gave him a smoke.[6]

He fell down, stretching, to become strong like a man and a woman. Having got strong, he sat up, he began to walk two feet up from the ground. So they said all right. He began to fly along the walls, like wind.

They said, "Think like a man."

So he said, "Ready."

They said, "Think like a woman. Look around all the place where we live."

So he went out and looked all around the town, like wind. So he saw the dead one. He could not meet him, he looked at him from all sides, he could not do anything to him. So he went back to the kiva.

"How did you go, father and our son?"

He said, "Yes, I saw him, but I do not know who he was. I could not meet him."

They were thinking about how to see and catch him. The next night, too, it was just the same. They gave him a smoke and he stretched and got strong, and sat up, and flew around the walls and went out.

They said, "Think like a man so you will catch it, whatever it is."

So he went around the town, and he saw that dead one. He ran away, he went on one side, he came on the other side, *all* night. He could not do anything. And he went into the kiva again.

"How did you go?" they asked him.

He said, "I saw a big one. I could not meet him. I think he is the one doing this. He is killing us all here. I think he is the one."

The next night he went again. They gave him a smoke and he stretched and got strong, and sat up, and flew around the walls and went out.

They said, "Think like a man so you will catch it, whatever it is."

So he went around the town, and he saw that dead one. He pretty nearly met him. All night he was chasing him. He went back to the kiva.

He said, "All the people in here, you must think about it good. I pretty nearly caught him."

The last night only the Outside chiefs and the old ones went in that kiva. They told the people to stay in their own houses. "There you can ask (pray to) our Father and Mother to catch him."

They gave him smoke, he got strong again, he stood up, he went up. He walked about only three times, not like other nights, and he went out and saw him. He turned, and met him.

He said, "My friend, is it you?"

"Yes, it is I."

"My friend, where do you live?"

He said, "I live way down here. Where do you live?"

"I live up there."

"Do you remember," he said, "once the fighting people came in here and we ran after them and some place way down there they killed me and they did not pick me up, they left me there and they did not make the four days for me or tell me to leave here. That is the one I am. I walked all around the world, I found no friends. So I came back here."[7]

"Just because you walk around I am here to talk with you. I am your friend."

"Let's go into this house," said the youth, "so you will know how I play with these people."

They were walking with *pinang*, so the people in the house did not hear them. This man was sleeping with his wife. He said, "Look at me." He put the straw into the girl's nostrils. She sneezed. He laughed. "That's the way I play," he said. He was going to tickle the man.

"Don't do it," said the youth. "Let's go out." They went out; they were talking.

"Let's go to my house." So his friend took him to his house. They went to the big hill, to the big stone; he turned it over the door. They went in; he covered it over again with the stone. He had everything in there—red beads, white beads, white dresses, black dresses, belts, buckskin, buffalo skin. "Look here, friend, I have got lots of things," he said. "Tomorrow night you must come, and we will play (gamble)."

So he said, "I guess I better go home." He went out, and went back to the kiva. He came in. The old men were just staying at talk there saying (i.e., praying), so he would catch it. The youth went in, he did not step anywhere on the ground, but went like wind. They asked him how he had fared, their son and father. He said, "I went and I know him, I have seen him."

"That is good! That is good! That is good!" they all said.[8] "Now you have to tell us about it," and they put him down in the middle and they sat around him, and he told them about it.

"Do you remember a long time ago they were coming into our town, fighting people, and some are living yet from that time. They ran after those warriors. They killed one man. Maybe you remember who he was. You did not pick him up. You left him. You did not make four days or anything for him. That is the one who walked around and then came back to his home. He is the one who is doing this. He walks at night into every house; he sticks the straw into their noses, they sneeze, and he laughs and the next morning they are dead. I met him. He said to me, 'My friend is here, and I walk around.' I said yes. He said to me, 'Let's go into this house.' A man there was sleeping with his wife. He began to tickle her with the straw. He laughed, he said, 'This is the way I play with these people. Those are they who die the next day.' That is what he did there. He said, 'Let's go into my house.' So he asked me to play (gamble) with him."

So he said to them he must get ready some red beads and turquoise (*konye*), and turquoise earrings (*konye oyekon*) and white garments and black garments. They went into their houses and got ready and made two large bundles. (That night his friend was to be waiting for him.)

He said to them, "When I say, 'get ready,' you must be ready, too, and call all the people into the kiva." So he said he was ready.

They got two Outside chiefs to go with him. He said to them, "When I go where that dead one lives, you just sit alongside on the road. When the dead one is about to beat me, and I am going to lose all my things, I will call up and you go in."

Their "Mothers" gave the Outside chiefs medicine, too. They carried his bundle. The dead one was waiting for him. He began to sound on the stone.

"My friend is coming," said the dead one, and he turned the stone. He threw in one bundle, and the other he carried. The Outside chiefs stayed up on top.

"I am coming with these bundles," he said. "I had a hard time; nobody helped me." He took out his things. The dead one said, "My friend, you are rich like me."

He said, "Yes."

They had a big fire. The dead one said, "Let's play *popoyoe´* (hidden ball)."

"No, let's not play *popoyoe´*, let's play with our hands."[9] He beat the dead one, the dead one had no chance.

He said, "Let's play with sticks."[10] The youth threw the sticks into the fire. So the dead one had to play with his hands. Then the dead one began to beat. Again the youth was beating. After a little they began to abuse each other. Then they laughed, then they got mad. The boy won all the things the dead one had.

He said, "Why did you put the ball in the fire? We ought to play with them now. You have won all my things," he said.

"Let's play again. I bet you all my things and the things I won from you, and do you bet me your heart."

They sang, they called it, they laughed. He won the heart. The dead one did not want to give his heart. They were pulling at each other's heart. Then he caught the dead one's heart in his left hand.[11] So he died, the second time. Twice he died. The youth took the heart and called the Outside chiefs and went into the kiva.

He said, "Now we shall have good times."

They tried to open his left hand. They could not open it. At last they opened it and they took the heart. And they told the dead one to go away from there, he did not belong there. That is how those Hopi people had *pinang*.[12] *Hu'!*

Notes

1. But the narrator was unable to give any explicit Hopi source. The ghost references are in general reminiscent of Maasewi, Skeleton, or Death, but that term was unfamiliar to the narrator.
2. Alcalde, two miles and a half from San Juan.
3. That is, they did not exorcise him.
4. Of fifteen or sixteen.
5. Presumably the road of meal to their altar.
6. In the long ritual pipe. Inferably there is a connection between smoking and *pinang*, as among the Tewa of Arizona. (See Robbins, Harrington, Freire-Marreco, 105.)
7. Cp. Dumarest, 170.
8. Just as Keresan ceremonialists would say to their messenger, "*Tauwa e.*" (That is good.)
9. The hands held palms up behind the back, the object to be guessed held in one hand.
10. Judging from parallel gaming bouts in other Pueblo folktales, the sticks were magical.
11. Elsewhere, also, the left hand is associated with death.
12. If they had had no *pinang*, they would not have caught the dead one.

Kuloskap and Pukjinskwes (1921)

(Passamaquoddy)

Recorder: John Dyneley Prince

There was a village of Indians; everyone, indeed, was a Black cat. One, however, the cleverest and bravest, goes off every day; he takes along his bow and arrows, axe and knife; he kills moose and bear; to the poor man he gives; he fed the poor. When he returns, they approach him to ask him where is what he has killed.

When he tells them, then they go off; their toboggans they fetch along; then they load them with meat. This is Pogumk the chief; his father (was) a bear. Pukjinskwes the witch was a she-Black cat. Woman or man she becomes according as she wishes, but in these days she is a man. Then she being evil; she hates the chief. A long time she considers how she can punish him and take away his place.

One day when they prepare what they have, they go to travel. Pukjinskwes says to the chief: "Come with me; we shall go to gather eggs." They go in a canoe. Again they canoe still farther. Then they come to an island. When they land, while he gathers eggs, Pukjinskwes then leaves him, going off in the canoe and she begins to sing: "I leave Pogumk on the island; now I am chieftain."

Then she comes to the village. In the morning all go to the woods; not one is left; he only who is worth most (?) (is not there). At night they camp. Every day they expect their chief. So then Pukjinskwes is chief.

On the thirteenth day the chief remembers his friend the fox who is a wizard or magician. Then he sings; the fox hears him, although he is far off. So he starts and goes to the island. When he finds the chief, at that time Pogumk cannot go (swim) far. The fox says to him that he will take him to the mainland; that they will go together by water. The fox says: "Close your eyes and seize my tail; do not fear; quickly we shall finally reach land."

Then his friend starts towing him (pulling); the chief begins to tire; a little he opens one eye, he sees that they are very near. He does not have faith. He thinks: "We shall never reach land." He says: "We shall never arrive."

The fox says to him: "Do not believe it."

But he thinks it very far. Pogumk thinks that he is scarcely strong enough, but so far as eye can reach (go), it is very stormy. The water indeed runs high. Pukjinskwes made it bad weather. All day they swim; not before it is dark do they land.

"My good friend," says Fox, "you may go." He runs to the Black cats' camp. When he comes to where they had been, only ashes are there and it is cold. The people had gone away. Then indeed he begins to follow them. In one day he comes near, he overtakes his mother carrying his younger brother, the Sable, on her back. She is looking ahead, but he (Sable) is looking backward.

As Pogumk comes out from the leaves, Sable sees him. He says: "My elder brother is following." When she turns, she does not see anything. Pogumk hides himself in a tree. Then they go on. Again Sable calls out: "Certainly my mother I see my elder brother." Then once more she turns; she catches him and they rejoice much and laugh. Then she throws Sable down on the leaves like a piece of wood.

Kuloskap instructs Sable: "Run to camp; when you come there, make a big fire, a hemlock bark fire, and throw into it Pukjinskwes's child; then do you come away quickly to me when you have done it."

What he had ordered, that was done. When the fire was hot, he throws the child into it; he burns it to death. Pukjinskwes is angry. Then she pursues him, as a wolf which is starving chases a rabbit.

Sable, very frightened, cries out: "My elder brother, my brother."

Pukjinskwes then screams out: "You must go as far as the island where Pogumk is, in order to save yourself." When this was said, Pogumk steps out to her from hiding; she sees him; then at once she is frightened. Then she loudly laughs; she says: "I was only chasing him in jest, because I like Sable."

But Pogumk answers her; he says: "I know you, and we know your devices, you evil demon." Then as his magic comes to him, he uses his power. Then he places Pukjinskwes with her back to a tree. Then she sticks fast to it; she cannot get away.

Sable and Kuloskap go away to the camp. This one, Pukjinskwes, has a stone hatchet and with great difficulty she cuts herself loose so that she can escape. Pogumk hears her pounding all night.

In the morning she comes to where they are; when they see her, she is carrying a piece of tree on her back; they scorn her and they sing at her: "This one leaves the thief on an island; now the chief sticks her fast to a tree."

Then Pukjinskwes the witch is mad (with shame) and insult; she departs forever from mankind; running wild like a vile wolf. She comes to Mount Desert; she sits on a log; she says: "Now I shall change myself into something to torture (mankind)." Then she cries out; she says: "A mosquito." Always even this day where Pogumk is, there Sable is also.

Now it is said that Pukjinskwes conceives children by Kiwakws, giants and monsters; her children are all ugly; she rears others' children; she can steal from other women their prettiest children; she rears them, as if they were her own children. That is so that she shall not be ashamed, so repulsive are her (own) children.

Once she had stolen a boy. Then someone asks him; he says: "That one is not your mother"; then he sees his sisters and his brothers, how ugly they are, like evil beasts. This then is their way, but he is handsome.

He asks his mother: "What does this mean?"

His mother answers him: "These were born in the night, but (?) you are a day child."

Mä'näbus Humbles a Chief's Son (1915)

(Menomini)

Recorders: Alanson Skinner and John V. Satterlee

Once Mä'näbus was disgusted with the son of a great chief because the youth was so arrogant. In order to take him down a peg, Mä'näbus secured the lights of an animal and made himself a vulva of them. Then he assumed the dress and form of a woman.

In this disguise Mä'näbus cast himself in the way of the young man and allowed himself to be seduced. He presently caught a little fox and keeping it under his dress he feigned pregnancy.

The chief's son was surprised at the unusual shortness of the period of gestation, but Mä'näbus assured him that something remarkable was about to happen. He pretended to lie in and feigned that he had given birth to the fox. In the midst of the chief's son's astonishment, Mä'näbus suddenly dragged forth the now putrid flesh that he had used as a vulva and threw it in the youth's face. "That is what you have been loving!" he cried and assumed his own shape.

The chief's son was covered with mortification.

The Mothway Myth (1978)

(Navaho)

Narrator: Slim Curly

Recorder: Berard Haile

This, it seems, (happened) also at the same Riverward Knoll.[1] Along its sunny side, in swampy places, (there are) beautiful flowers which are white in season. There it seems that White Butterfly (Moth) originated, and red moths of various colors had originated there, they say. Along its slope, the plants were large and their tips (blossoms were) white. As they were of both sexes, I suppose, it happened that the Sun looked at them time and again. At their (flowery) tips, it seems, their female organ happened to be, and at the tips (of others were) their male organs. Here, after these (plants) were put in this condition, the Begochidi-to-be was born.

This one, it seems, began to go about here. When those Butterfly People[2] had been born, a number of whom I suppose were of the same parents, he began to stay among them taking them in his care. Some of these were boys, some girls, (and) he would put his hand to their crotches saying "be-go be-go"—as he was a berdache. Right there, it seems, he raised the Butterfly People, young men and young women in large numbers, taking care of them, encircling them all the time and never letting them out of his sight. It seems that he knew a report that somewhere along the mountain range, people were hunting, (because) he traveled there with the haze, they say. So immediately he traveled by haze. There, it seems, whenever they would crawl upon deer, and at the moment they wanted to shoot, he would feel their lower parts from behind and say "bego" to them. On that account, the game would be missed, and it was unpleasant (hunting).

Then too, when marrying was done and the two would lie down and were about to have intercourse, he would touch the lower parts of both parties and say "bego." It was simply everywhere that he did this, they say. Even if a woman wanted to urinate and would squat for that, he would touch her lower parts and say "bego." And even to men he did likewise. So it seems that Bego did this and, according to this saying that he has touched somebody's crotch, he was called Bego-chidi.[3] By a change of colors, the (same) haze moved about with him, they say. The same person they called "Bego-who-touches," "Bego-who-is-white," "Bego-who-is-black," "Bego-who-is-yellow," they say.

In this manner it seems that he appeared everywhere, along the mountain ranges, along the water courses, or wherever Holy People dwelt. He had in his possession the so-called "earth mirage (stone)," they say, (also) rock mirage, tree mirage, plant mirage, and rising haze (heat waves).[4] So it seems that large numbers of maidens, as said, were raised at that place. If from various places it were said: "Let him be married to her," he would say: "No, no," as he would shake his finger and refuse to part from her. Neither would he part from the young men. So whenever it was said concerning maidens of different places: "Let him be married to her," he would say: "No, no." And whenever it was said of a youth: "He shall marry at this and that place," he would say: "No," as he walked in their protection. Only he himself would go among them when they would lie down to sleep, saying "Bego bego" as he put his hands to their crotches.

Meanwhile, it seems, it was said that over on the Wide-belt Mesa side, game of every different shade existed. Beginning with elk and ending down the line with the cottontail, their (existence) suddenly became known to this extent, while Begochidi, it seems, immediately got restless, they say. "I shall be there," he said and immediately left on his haze waves in that direction toward the Wide-belt Mesa. There the crowd of those Butterfly People had moved this way to the red-streaked slope where, it seems, a discussion was held. Dark Butterfly, with wings so wide and the kind with a white border at their edges, was made the very first chief. Next to him, the one with very wide, white wings, the edges of which are somewhat black bordered, was also made a chief. Next to this one, the yellow one, whose wing borders are sort of black streaked, was made third place chief. In the fourth place, they put the red one as chief, whose (wing) edges are black streaked. All told, there was a large number of them.

And so it seems that right around there, many bugs of various kinds had their homes. From elsewhere, people were asking for them in vain. Whenever one was asked: "Let him be married to that maiden," they were (refused because of Begochidi). "No, you must know that she was nursed by me. I raised her, therefore I love her much and do not care at all to give her to another person," they (their parents under the influence of Begochidi) were saying. In this manner, these maidens had been raised in great numbers.

After that had happened, it seems they again began to move camp from there and move over to Hopi. Then it seems that they were gathering herb pollen along moist places as that was their only food. In the morning, they would spread out for that, and in the late afternoon, they would meet at home (again), while at night they themselves would care for each other. Then it seems that the appointed chiefs would ask: "Are you all returned now? Are your numbers complete?"

"Yes, all of us have returned; we are in full number, not one of us is absent," the answer would be.

"Besides, from places you are being asked in marriage, you say! This is your affair. You (the mothers) who have given birth to them, and you (the fathers) who have daughters, you yourselves have the say in this."

"What shall I say (about it)? It is all right with me!"

"With me also," "With me too," "With me too," they would say. The chiefs who had been appointed would speak, one following the other.

After that it seems that those whose children they were, would speak: "Even so, my Chief! As for me, when I think of this, is it for a man who has been raised in some other place that a person (his wife) is nursing his baby (daughter) here? And after having raised it, what an awful thing it would be should one give her to a man elsewhere!" they would say.

"Therefore I do not want to do that! I, too, think likewise," those were saying whose children had been asked in marriage, as they would speak up.

From there it seems they again moved camp this way. At that point of Black Mesa which hooks (like a fin), below which a place is called Fish-flows-out, there they again moved camp. Having made a brush circle, they would build fires inside of it and make that their home for the time being. Right there it seems that they were again living.

Exclusively for nice flowers they would go out and then return here again. "Have you all returned now? Is anyone of you absent?"

"Yes, all of us have returned."

So it usually would be done, they say. Besides, asking in marriage is being done from (various) places they say, (but) that was refused. "That is the proper thing, no doubt of it!" Only this they would tell one another, they say.

As time passed, in the course of a single day, from fifty and sixty places, useless requests for marriage had come to be made. From there it seems they again began to move camp, and at that Chinle place, there happened to be many cottonwood catkins. Here they acted much as though they were thrown in (there); they sat down and got busy with them. Immediately, I suppose, around there, marriage proposals were made to those maidens. Even then, it seems, those who were uselessly asking marriage would tell those chiefs, they say.

Then it seems that at sunset they made camp opposite White House. A brush circle was even made of Beeweed, and fires were built with some Greasewood.

Shortly after sunset, it seems, when the evening twilight was still strung out, the chief said as before: "Are you all here? Isn't anyone of you absent?"

"No, not one of us is missing. It seems all of us are here," the answer was.

"Count one another carefully!" they were told.

"We did count one another. Our numbers are complete! Not one of us is absent," the reply was, they say.

"Along all those places where fires have been built, let each one of you, wherever you may be now, sit down and be all ears! You must listen! I shall now speak to you!" said he who was chief. When some time had passed he asked: "Are you all now seated properly?"

"Yes, yes, we are properly seated," they said.

Now he was standing as he spoke: "If one of you thinks 'I shall now speak,' you must arise and you may speak while you stand. To do so while you are sitting will not be recognized!" he said. "Is this what I am saying: 'Now I want to speak to you,' is this agreed? Is it all right?" he asked.

Immediately it seems one of them arose somewhere, holding up his hand. "Yes it is certainly all right! Do speak to us!" he said.

"Now regarding this of which I want to speak, if satisfactory to you, you will say, 'That is good, it seems,' if not, you will say, 'That is not satisfactory to us at all.' So either way is very agreeable to me," he said.

After that it seems (he began): "Yonder at the place where we used to live, this Begochidi, as you know, raised you, being your aunt, your uncle, your granduncle," he said. "Besides (he) loving you very much, you (were) having a great love for him," he said. "Now at that same place, whenever you were asked for marriage uselessly because he (your suitor) said 'No' and you were saying 'No,' that won out as the rule, which from then till now has (been practiced). From there, to your misfortune, he (Begochidi) left for Wide-belt Mesa where he is again busy with the same kind of work," he said. "Now whatever the reason may have been why he used to take care of you, the fact is that to this day, you are guided by him in refusing (marriage)," he said to them. "Now as I think of it, all those of you who are men would have taken him for your wife, that is clear, because he had very much love for you and you had great love for him. All of you who are women, he would have taken for wives. You see, you loved him greatly and he loved you greatly. Where is there another like him that you could take?" he said to them. "Therefore, on that account, he raised you at the time. You who are on the men's side, by feeling around from time to time for the bulk and size of your penises. Likewise you on the women's side he used to feel around your vaginas for that same purpose. But that (marriage with him) did not come to pass. He has gone somewhere and has stayed away from you. Is that not a fact? How does it look to you?" he asked, they say.

"That is really so. We used to love him very much and he too used to love us," they said, every one of them. "Besides, along the places where we moved, we have been asked ever so many times in vain (for marriage), and the same continues here where we have camped."

"I wonder how it is that I am thinking," he said. "Now the truth is, that at the time you became pregnant with those children, no help came to you in any way from those places from which their marriage is (now) offered to you, but you became pregnant with them and you gave birth to them and you nursed them (yourselves). So it is true, you love them much, I think, in that way I am thinking about you. What about you? What do you think?" he said.

"That's just the thing! It's the real truth!" Such words were said as the crowd rose, they say.

"Now some of you have two children, some even four, but these you love greatly and they love one another," he said. "So who would marry you? And that is the truth, your daughter would be one place somewhere and your son would be another place, but you would be crying for them," he said. "So this coming evening your children—some of whom are boys, some girls, those that love each other—shall prepare their bedding for one another. They shall lie together. Every one of them you must place under one another's cover. That alone will be a good thing in my opinion, because you love your children and they themselves love one another. Only that will be good, I think. How does it appeal to you?" he asked them.

And then the chief who was second in rank (said): "I am of the same opinion. It appeals to me," he said.

The chief who was next in rank said likewise and the very last one in rank said: "Are these the only ones that will be in this condition? All of these that live on Earth will do that, I suppose," he said, they say.

Now it so happened that the children of Dawn, who were brothers and sisters, were present there. "We also shall do this," they said, it was learned. Then it seems that after dark (they asked): "Is it now?"

"Yes, now is the time," was the reply.

The beddings were then prepared, it seems. Those of the same parents lay down together, they say. After this had happened, they were copulating till morning. On the following morning, everybody (seemed) happy as moving again began, and brother and sisters had their arms around each other. From there they (moved) below Rock Fall, then to Black Rock, and up out of the canyon to the rim.

Here, it seems, along the base of Black Rock, four fires some distance apart were built, they say. Then it seems they (the Moth People) rushed into those fires one on top of the other, burning themselves up. They simply tramped over each other from all sides in a mad rush to get into the fire.

Then it seems that those who were chiefs extinguished the fire. After that they went wild as though they had drunk whisky. On that side (somewhere), one of those that were "inner forms" of mountains, had, among others, gotten into this condition and, catching fire, had burnt up, they say. And another smooth Rock Ledge was made to extend out between them; it was made so that they could not see one another, (after which) they quieted down on both sides. News of this was then spread in all directions. There is nobody, they said, none that knows (a cure) for a condition like this. Therefore there is absolutely a mutual fear of their lower parts between brothers and sisters. The mere thought of such a thing is to be feared. This became known at that place.

It was found, however, that Coyote alone had medicine for (incest) cases of this kind. News was then sent to Big-water (Mountain), it seems. "You must realize, I may be able to do something; I am somewhat familiar with such cases," said the Big Bear Man. "For that, the male and female generative organs of coyotes of one litter are used,[5] also the male and female organs of Yellow Foxes of one litter are used, that happens to be (what is needed)," they say.

And the same parts of Blue Fox are used, and those of Badgers of one litter, and of Bear of the same litter. And of Moth medicines there were four, it was learned.[6] For that purpose it seems that a hogan was built at that place, which is the Tapering Sandhill that sets farthest away from here.[7] Then the medicines referred to were set in the fire, and when they were well boiled, the said collected penises were thrown in, after which the Fire Ceremony was held. After he had made them a dress of a coyote hide (and clothed them in it), they drank it. It seems it was the Dawn Children, brother and sister mentioned before, for whom the ceremony was conducted. With their buttocks touching one another, they vomited opposite one another. With a splashing sound, they threw up the moths at either side. Using the pokers, they threw this (refuse) into the fire, they say.

Bear Man, I suppose, was conducting the ceremony at the time. From somewhere, the Wind People came, driving along the Butterflies who were sort of out of their minds. Staggering about any old way, they came swaying along to that place. And when they had driven them around the fire four times, they began to rush out through the smoke hole. That was all that happened, and in this manner it seems that the ceremony was held here. That story ends right there. This, it seems, was the rule which the Big Bear Man laid down for himself at the time. When two are born together (brother and sister), one went into the interior of the Tapering Sandhill which stands on this (the Wheatfield) side, while on the farther one (Whisky Creek) there is now a home.[8]

"Whenever, in the future, Mothway (power) causes (danger of) death, these particular four herbs shall be the main ones and all (other) herbs may, without one exception, be gathered (and used)," he said. "For the Prostitution (Copulation) Way also, even though it has tobacco, its smoke shall also be prepared with these same 'around-it herbs' which are plucked,"[9] he said, they say.

That is all that happened, I suppose. Here this story of Mothway ends.[10]

Notes

1. Riverward Knoll is a small hill, a few miles southwest of Holbrook, Arizona (Fr. Berard). The editor has searched this area. No conspicuous hill is located in this general region. A few eligible hillocks are now built over by settlers who try to escape the flood waters of the Little Colorado River. This suggests that to early Navajo visitors the Riverward Knoll vegetation was more important than the geological feature.
2. No distinction seems to be made in the story between Butterfly and Moth.
3. Accordingly his name would signify "the bego who touches." "Bego" by itself seems to have no meaning, as far as I can learn. The "touch," as described in the text, seems to have been borne out in the low-toned *chid,* with high-toned relative *i,* although some informants also give *chíd* a high tone.

Another interpretation of this being is given in the story of "Creation of Game" by James Smith. See Luckert, *The Navajo Hunter Tradition*, 1975, 96ff. There are still others who assign the guardianship of the universe to Begochidi, a position which is difficult to reconcile with the one assigned to him here. Up to the present stage of writing, I am inclined to accept the interpretation which is offered in this account—"bego who touches."[Begochidi of this myth and Begochiddy of Hasteen Klah's "The Story of the Emergence," which I've included in this volume, are the same individuals. —JE]

4. Haze signifies here heat and cold waves. The mirage of various names probably has reference to his power to cause mirage phenomena in which stones, trees, etc. appear enlarged.
5. The text uses "those born together" which is a common expression for brothers and sisters, or for "children of the same parents." In this instance I have used "litter" for this.
6. These herbs are not mentioned by name.
7. This would be the tapering sand hill near Whisky Creek.
8. The sentence seems to be inserted and interrupts the narrative which speaks of the rule laid down by Big Bear Man. The sentence is not quite clear, but our informant wishes to say that the brothers and sisters were assigned to the two tapering hills which are now their homes. The rule laid down concerning incest is quoted in the following sentences.
9. The herbs "around" are any herb gathered at large. Any and all of these may be added to the tobacco which is the chief requisite in the Prostitution Way ceremony.
10. The account considers only incest between brothers and sisters which, in popular belief, still leads to insanity. While *iich'aah* is the name for the moth, it also signifies insanity which follows marriage between close blood relatives, as well as the ceremony which is required to right such a condition. As clan relatives are brothers and sisters, the marriage between closely related clan members is incestuous. Such a relationship, our informant explains, extends even to distant clan relatives on the father's side. Clan brothers and sisters therefore should not shake hands with one another. A sister should not hand a brother anything in the way of food, bedding and the like, but should place this on the floor, where the brother may help himself. While these and similar rules, such as mentioning a clan relative's name, are not strictly observed by the younger generation, there are not a few of the older generation that observe them most conscientiously, both among men and women. As for employing the *ajilee* in enticing women, our informant opines that the practice is no longer common. Once the ceremony was performed over a woman, she was considered immune; no prayer, song, or footprint drawing could again take effect on her. This rule and the clan relationship clearly defined the limits of prostitution.

Nih'ā^{n}ça^{n} and Panther-Young-Man (1903)

(Arapaho)

Narrator: "J"

Recorders: George A. Dorsey and Alfred L. Kroeber

Nih'ā^{n}ça^{n} lived with his wife and children. He asked his wife: "Are there any young men who come to the tent courting?"

She told him: "Yes, there is one. His name is Panther-young-man (*bäxa^{n} kä̆^{n}anaxaä*)."

Nih'ā^{n}ça^{n} dressed himself as a woman, and went out for water. The Panther saw and approached him. At first Nih'ā^{n}ça^{n} seemed not to notice him. Then he smiled at him. The Panther asked him to marry him, and Nih'ā^{n}ça^{n} consented. So they were married and lived together.

Nih'ā^{n}ça^{n} told the Panther: "Only touch me, that will satisfy you."

He sent him hunting. Then he went out on the prairie. He saw a rabbit, and said: "Come here, my friend, I wish to speak to you."

"What do you wish?" asked the rabbit.

"I want you for my child. I will keep you and give you food and water." The rabbit consented, and Nih'ā^{n}ça^{n} took him home under his dress.

After a time, when the Panther came home, he said to him: "We are going to have a child."

"Good," said the Panther. He continued to go hunting.

The rabbit grew fat, and Nih'ā^{n}ça^{n} became tired of caring for him, feeding him, and giving him drink. So he gave birth, and wrapped the rabbit up closely, and laid him on his bed. When the Panther came home, he told him: "We have had a child born to us."

"Good," said the Panther. "Is it a boy or a girl?"

"A boy," said Nih'ā^{n}ça^{n}. "That is good."

"It is very strange in appearance. It looks like a rabbit. It is very fat."

"It is well," said the Panther. Then he started out to hunt again, but came back behind the tent and listened.

A man from another tent came in and said to Nih'ā^{n}ça^{n}: "It is very strange. You have been married only a short time, and have a child already. How can that be?"

"This is how it is," said Nih'ā^{n}ça^{n}, opening his dress et penem stantem monstrans.[1] "That is how I gave birth to a child."

When the Panther heard this, he ran into the timber (from shame).

"Stay there! The woods and brush will be where you live," Nih'ā^{n}ça^{n} said to him. Then he said to the rabbit: "You are too fat. You shall have no fat, except on your kidneys, and on your back behind the shoulders. You will run fast, and leap, and live on the prairie. This I give to you."

Note

1. Nih'ā^{n}ça^{n} showed the neighbor man his erect penis. —JE

Pleiades and Taurus (1940)

(Yokut)

Narrator: Sam Osborn

Recorders: A.H. Gayton and Stanley S. Newman

The Waksachi version of this tale is localized at Koiwuniu, a large rock on a hill above Adam's Flat. Now among the Waksachi who were living at a village in the flat were seven young wives and their husbands. One of these women was smaller than the others; another one had a child. These women were homosexual and daily went off together to picnic on Koiwuniu, while their husbands were out hunting.

It was spring; clover and wild onion were beginning to grow. The young women did not know how to avoid their husbands who were not attractive to them. When it came time to go home, they rubbed wild onion on their mouths. That night when they went to bed all the husbands were repulsed by the odor and told their wives to turn over the other way or go to sleep elsewhere. The girls pretended indignation and the next day went to their parents' homes. But they were at once sent back to their men, being told to go and eat with them. They went home and fed their men meat and mush, but they did not eat with them. They kept this up for six days and ate no food; they were planning to leave their men permanently.

On the last day they all went up the hill again. Each of them had eagle-down ropes; these were their talismans. The next day they went up the hill again, but on the way up, the youngest girl's nose began to bleed. She asked the others to wait for her. She sat down to rest and her friends sang to her. She turned to stone. She can still be seen sitting there. A little stream of water flows out of her stone nose; those who have tasted it say that it is bitter.

Then the rest went on up to the large rock. They laid out all their talismans in a single line and stood on them. They stood in a row, all facing the same way. The mother had brought her little girl with her. Then the ringleader of the group threw her eagle-down rope up in the sky; it caught in the center so that both ends hung down to the ground. These ends the woman tied around the ropes on the ground. She tied it right at the middle. Then the girls all clasped hands, called upon their talismans to help them, and began to sing. Slowly the ropes on which they were standing began to rise and swing slowly round and round like a buzzard. It swung in bigger and bigger circles. They sailed over their village and their parents saw them. The people below rushed out with beads and belts to try and bribe the girls to come down, but to no avail. The husbands saw their wives up there and scolded their parents-in-law for letting the girls get away.

Now the men had eagle-rope talismans just like their wives, and they decided to follow. They ran up the hill and saw the stone woman sitting there; they knew what had happened to her. They put down their ropes as the girls had done and were soon sailing out in the sky and over the village. Again the old people came out and begged their sons to come back. By this time, the women had reached the spot in the sky where we see them now. They looked back and saw their men coming after them. They talked about whether or not they should let them come on. But they stood by their first plan: they wanted to be alone in the sky. As soon as the men got close enough, the girls shouted to them to stop right where they were. There they stayed and you can see them now a little way back of their wives. They did not want to go home again.[1]

Note

1. Sam Osborn says that the Michahai, Waksachi, Choinimni, Wobonuch, and Patwisha all tell this story; each version is localized at a rock in their territory.

The footprints of the women may be seen on all the rocks. The Michahai and others call the constellation representing the husbands Young Men. The Pleiades are called Young Women.

Related Myths and Legends for Further Reading

"Beaver Origin Legend" [Second Version]. William Whitman. *The Oto.* New York: AMS, 1969. 29.

"Beginnings of the Universe." Matilda Coxe Stevenson. *The Zuñi Indians: Their Mythology, Esoteric Fraternities, and Ceremonies.* U.S. Bureau of Ethnology *Annual Report* 11 (1889–90): 23–24.

"The Beheaded Ones." George A. Dorsey and Alfred L. Kroeber. *Traditions of the Arapaho.* Field Museum of Natural History, Anthropological Series, 5. Chicago: Field Museum, 1903. 133–35.

"Biography of Woman Chief." Edwin T. Denig. *Of the Crow Nation.* Smithsonian Institution, Bureau of American Ethnology, *Bulletin* 151, no. 33 (1953): 64–68.

"The Birth of the Old Ones or Ancients of the Kâ´kâ." Frank Hamilton Cushing. *Outlines of Zuñi Creation Myths.* Smithsonian Institution, Bureau of American Ethnology, *Annual Report* 13 (1891–1892, 1896): 401–3.

Bowers, Alfred W. *Hidasta Social and Ceremonial Organization.* Smithsonian Institution, Bureau of American Ethnology, *Bulletin* 194 (1965): 252–57.

"The Brothers, the Sister, and the Red Bird." James Owen Dorsey. *The Cegiha Language.* Department of the Interior, U.S. Geographical and Geological Survey of the Rocky Mountain Region. *Contributions to North American Ethnology* 6 (1890): 224–26.

"Chicken Hawk and Toad." Franz Boas. *Kutenai Tales.* Smithsonian Institution, Bureau of American Ethnology, *Bulletin* 59 (1918): 43.

"Coyote and Wolf." Robert H. Lowie. "Shoshonean Tales." *Journal of American Folk-Lore* 37, no. 1 (Jan.–June 1924): 212–13.

"Coyote Tricks Cougar Into Providing Food," "Tales." *The Sinkaietk or Southern Okanagon of Washington*. Ed. Leslie Spier. Menasha, WI: George Banta, 1938. 232–33.

"The Creation of Game Animals." Karl W. Luckert. *The Navajo Hunter Tradition*. Tucson: University of Arizona Press, 1975. 21–22.

"Creation of the Sun and Moon." Aileen O'Bryan. *The Dîné: Origin Myths of the Navajo Indians*. Smithsonian Institution, Bureau of American Ethnology, *Bulletin* 163 (1956): 14–16.

"The Creation or Age of Beginning." Aileen O'Bryan. *The Dîné: Origin Myths of the Navajo Indians*. Smithsonian Institution, Bureau of American Ethnology, *Bulletin* 163 (1956): 1–13.

"Cuna′waBl′s Grandson." Robert H. Lowie, "Shoshonean Tales." *Journal of American Folk-Lore* 37, no. 1 (Jan.–June 1924): 165–67.

Devereux, George. "Institutionalized Homosexuality of the Mohave Indians." *Human Biology* 9 (1937): 498–527.

"The Disobedient Brother." Robert H. Lowie. *The Northern Shoshone*. American Museum of Natural History, *Anthropological Papers* 2.3 (1909): 287–88.

"Double-Face Tricks the Girl." Ella Deloria. *Dakota Texts*. American Ethnological Society, *Publications* 14 (1932): 49–50.

"Elk Gens." William Whitman. *The Oto*. New York: AMS, 1969. 30.

"The Emergence." Elsie Clews Parsons. *Tewa Tales*. New York: Kraus, 1969. 9–15.

"False Friend." Elsie Clews Parsons. *Tewa Tales*. New York: Kraus, 1969. 36–38.

Fletcher, Alice C., and Francis la Flesche. *The Omaha Tribe*. Smithsonian Institution, Bureau of American Ethnology, *Annual Report* 27 (1905–1906, 1911): 132–33.

"Foot-Stuck-Child" [First Version]. George A. Dorsey and Alfred L. Kroeber. *Traditions of the Arapaho*. Field Museum of Natural History, Anthropological Series, 5. Chicago: Field Museum, 1903. 153–59.

"Foot-Stuck-Child" [Second Version]. George A. Dorsey and Alfred L. Kroeber. *Traditions of the Arapaho*. Field Museum of Natural History, Anthropological Series, 5. Chicago: Field Museum, 1903. 160–61.

Goddard, Pliny Earle. *Navajo Texts*. Ed. Gladys A. Reichard. American Museum of Natural History, *Anthropological Papers* 34, part 1 (1933): 128–29.

"Good-for-Nothing." Kaj Birket-Smith and Frederica de Laguna. *The Eyak Indians of the Copper River Delta, Alaska.* Koberhavn: Levin & Munksgaard, 1938. 316–17.

"He Follows His Dead Wife." Elsie Clews Parsons. *Tewa Tales.* New York: Kraus, 1969. 22–24.

Hill, W. W. *Navajo Agricultural and Hunting Methods.* Yale University, *Publications in Anthropology* 18 (1938): 99, 123.

Hill, W. W. "Note on the Pima Berdache." *American Anthropologist,* n.s. 40 (1938): 339.

"How Coyote Went to Get Basket Weaving Twigs." Carobeth Laird. *Mirror and Pattern: George Laird's World of Chemehuevi Mythology.* Banning, CA: Malki Museum Press, 1984. 49–58.

"In the Beginning." Stanley A. Fishler. *In the Beginning: A Navajo Creation Myth.* Department of Anthropology, University of Utah, *Anthropological Papers,* no. 13 (Jan. 1953): 9–26.

"The Indian Devil, the Mischief Maker." John Dyneley Prince. *Passamaquoddy Texts.* Publications of the American Ethnological Society, 10. New York: Stechert, 1921. 58–77.

"The Killing of the Five Brothers from Kangiaq." Kaj Birket-Smith. *The Cugach Eskimo.* Kobenhavn: Nationalmuseets, 1953. 136–37.

Klah, Hasteen. *Hail Chant and Water Chant.* Mary C. Wheelwright, Recorder. Navajo Religion Series 2. Santa Fe: Museum of Navajo Ceremonial Art, 1946. 3–16.

Luckert, Karl W. *The Navajo Hunter Tradition.* Tucson: University of Arizona Press, 1975. 96–121.

Matthews, Washington. *Navajo Legends.* New York: Kraus, 1969. 77–78, 86–87.

"Navajo Origin Legend." A. M. Stephen. *Journal of American Folk-Lore* 43 (1930): 88–102.

"Nih'ā^{n}ça^{n} Disguises Himself as a Woman." George A. Dorsey and Alfred L. Kroeber. *Traditions of the Arapaho.* Field Museum, *Anthropological Series* 5 (Oct. 1903): 71–72.

"The Origin Myth of Zuñi." Elsie Clews Parsons. *Journal of American Folk-Lore* 36 (Apr.–June 1923): 135–62.

"Pah-Hah-Undootah the Red Head." *The Myth of Hiawatha and Other Oral Legends, Mythologic and Allegoric, of the North American Indians.* Henry R. Schoolcraft. Philadelphia: Lippincott, 1856. 216–22.

Reichard, Gladys A. *Navaho Religion: A Study of Symbolism*. Vol. 1. Bollingen Series 18. New York: Pantheon, 1950. 41–42, 309, 387–88.

"The Revenge of the Sky People." Leo J. Frachtenberg. *Coos Texts.* Columbia University Contributions to Anthropology, 1. New York: Columbia University, 1913. 149, 151, 153, 155, 157.

"The Road-Woman (Bo´-hem-kül´-leh)." Stephen Powers. *Tribes of California.* Berkeley: University of California Press, 1976. 345.

"Scalp Dance." George Bird Grinnell. *The Cheyenne Indians: Their History and Ways of Life.* Vol. 2. New York: Cooper Station, 1962. 39–44.

"Second Bear Origin Legend." William Whitman. *The Oto.* New York: AMS , 1969. 22–23.

"Splinter-Foot-Girl." George A. Dorsey and Alfred L. Kroeber. *Traditions of the Arapaho.* Field Museum, *Anthropological Series* 5 (Oct. 1903): 161–78.

"Spring-Boy and Lodge-Boy." Martha Warren Beckwith. *Mandan-Hidatsa Myths and Ceremonies.* New York: Kraus, 1969. 30–43.

Stevenson, Matilda Coxe. *The Sia.* U.S. Bureau of American Ethnology, *Annual Report* 23 (1901–2): 40–69.

Stirling, Matthew W. *Origin Myth of Acoma and Other Records.* Smithsonian Institution, Bureau of American Ethnology, *Bulletin* 135 (1942): 70.

"The Story of Bekotsidi." Washington Matthews. *Navajo Myths, Prayers, and Songs with Texts and Translations.* Ed. Pliny Earle Goddard. University of California, *Publications in American Archaeology and Ethnology* 5.2 (n.d.): 58–60.

"The Story of Hemataxceyó-evonhotoxc (Brittle Bow Star)." Warren E. Schwartz. *The Last Contrary: The Story of Wesley Whiteman (Black Bear).* Sioux Falls, SD: Center for Western Studies, Augustana College, 1989. 88–89.

"The Story of Wisa'kä." William Jones. *Fox Texts.* American Ethnological Society, *Publications* 1 (1907): 337–39.

"The Sun Boys." Robert H. Lowie. "Shoshonean Tales." *Journal of American Folk-Lore* 37, no. 1 (Jan.–June 1924): 190–91.

"The Sun's Dead Sons." Carobeth Laird. *Mirror and Pattern: George Laird's World of Chemehuevi Mythology.* Banning, CA: Malki Museum Press, 1984. 204–7.

"Tender-Foot Woman." George A. Dorsey and Alfred L. Kroeber. *Traditions of the Arapaho*. Field Museum, *Anthropological Series* 5 (Oct. 1903): 179–80.

"The Three Siblings." Robert H. Lowie. "Shoshonean Tales." *Journal of American Folk-Lore* 37, no. 1 (Jan.–June 1924): 136–42.

"Transvestites." Leslie Spier. *Klamath Ethnography*. Berkeley: University of California Press, 1930. 51–53.

"The Traveling Woman." Robert H. Lowie. "Shoshonean Tales." *Journal of American Folk-Lore* 37, no. 1 (Jan.–June 1924): 177–79.

"Where People Moved Opposite." Berard Haile. *Women Versus Men: A Conflict of Navajo Emergence; The Curly Tó Aheedlíinii Version*. Ed. Karl W. Luckert. Lincoln: University of Nebraska Press, 1981. 13–32.

"White Plum Boy." Ella C. Deloria. *Dakota Texts*. American Ethnological Society, *Publications* 14 (1932): 106–13.

"Wolf's Grandson and the Sky Boys." Robert H. Lowie. "Shoshonean Tales." *Journal of American Folk-Lore* 37, no. 1 (Jan.–June 1924): 124–18.

"Women and War." George Bird Grinnell. *The Cheyenne Indians: Their History and Ways of Life*. Vol. 2. New York: Cooper Station, 1962. 44–47.

Zigmond, Maurice. "The Spiritual World of the Kawaiisu." *Flowers of the Wind: Papers on Ritual, Myth and Symbolism in California and the Southwest*. Ed. Thomas C. Blackburn. Socorro, NM: Ballena, 1977. 74.

Title Index

Index to Tribes and Nations